At the WATER'S EDGE

At the WATER'S EDGE

SUMMER ESCAPES FOR EASY LIVING

SALLY HAYDEN

photography by **EARL CARTER**

LONDON · NEW YORK

Senior Designer Barbara Zuñiga
Commissioning Editor Annabel Morgan
Location Research Jess Walton
Production Director Patricia Harrington
Art Director Leslie Harrington
Editorial Director Julia Charles

First published in 2013
by Ryland Peters & Small
20–21 Jockey's Fields
London WC1R 4BW
and
519 Broadway, 5th Floor
New York, NY 10012

www.rylandpeters.com

10 9 8 7 6 5 4 3 2 1

LONDON • NEW YORK

ISBN 978 1 84975 358 6

A catalogue record for this book is available from the
British Library.

US Library of Congress cataloging-in-publication data has
been applied for.

Printed in China

CONTENTS

introduction

I was lucky enough to grow up in Australia, where my family had a holiday home by the sea. When we arrived there at the start of each summer, a sense of deep calm would instantly take hold. The light-filled, open-plan interiors, offering the illusion of endless space, were complemented by a large and beautiful garden that overlooked the nearby beach. This was the start of my lifelong love of coastal living.

I am still inspired today by informal, laid-back living spaces. Cool, calming colours, natural materials, whitewashed floors and soft flowing linens are all indispensable elements of such interiors, but so too is a robust practicality. These are spaces that allow us to be completely relaxed and carefree.

This book is a celebration of waterside homes and their eternal appeal. It showcases houses in remarkable locations with interesting architecture and gorgeous interiors that are sure to delight and inspire. It also looks at design features that play an key role in waterside homes, and illustrates how and why these elements enhance the experience of living by the water.

These beautiful homes from across the globe celebrate the timeless allure of living by the water. Each home has its own take on the informal simplicity of seaside style and showcases a multitude of inspiring ideas and insights that can be translated to any home, whether it is beside the water or not.

OPPOSITE ABOVE LEFT: In a coastal home, a collection of vintage wooden floats and other maritime paraphernalia makes visual reference to the nearby beach.

OPPOSITE ABOVE RIGHT: A bicycle stand at the front entrance of this Fire Island home provides a hint as to the island's main mode of summertime transport.

OPPOSITE BELOW LEFT: Weathered wood and coiled rope offer textural inspiration for a home at the water's edge.

OPPOSITE BELOW RIGHT: One of the joys of summer living by the sea is eating outside. Here, all the necessary equipment for eating alfresco is kept close to hand in this covered entrance area.

PART 1

Inspirations

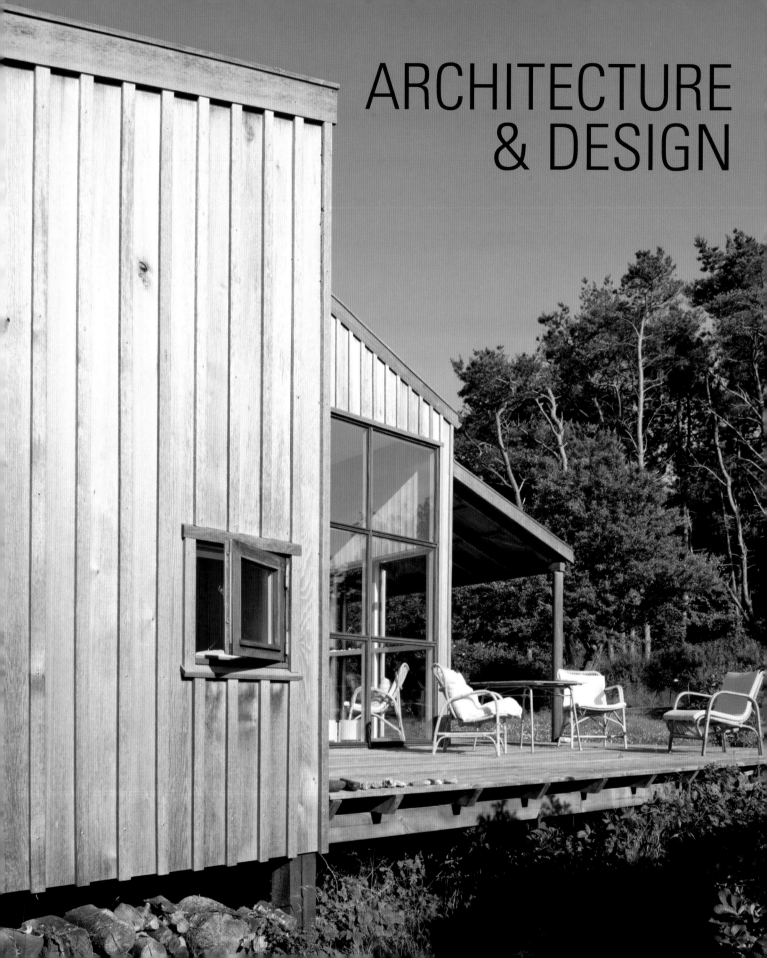

ARCHITECTURE
& DESIGN

common design elements

Ranging from sumptuous modern villas to shacks in the sand dunes, waterside homes come in a great variety of architectural forms.

The style of a waterside house will frequently depend on the architectural traditions of the country or region it is situated in, and can vary from traditional wooden houses with gabled roofs and exposed beams to modern structures that are all clean lines, glass and metal. Whatever the architectural style, the building materials must be selected to withstand the harsh climatic conditions of a coastal location.

When it comes to planning and designing a home near the water, the main consideration is to create a dwelling that works well with the local environment and the surrounding landscape.

Orientating the house to take advantage of any views, creating a spacious and relaxing outdoor area and optimizing natural light are all important. That is why beach or waterside houses so often include large picture windows, sliding and French doors, balconies, decks, terraces, porches or verandahs – all of which help the occupants to make the most of the pleasures of coastal living. Using materials that reflect the natural maritime environment is another key aspect of successful seaside design.

Coastal and waterside homes are designed for enjoyment and relaxation, so they should also be practical. It is a good idea to keep things casual and low maintenance by selecting finishes that are easy to live with and easy to look after.

OPPOSITE: Simple materials such as glass and wood, combined with clean architectural lines, ensure that this modern summerhouse effortlessly integrates with the surrounding landscape.

RIGHT: The gabled roof is characteristic of traditional Danish cabins. This modern example has a deep overhang to provide shade and shelter for the deck.

layout & planning

Houses near water are more often than not places for escape from everyday life. They are also usually designed to accommodate gatherings of family and friends in an informal environment. Accordingly, the layout should reflect these different roles.

Open-plan living is well suited to waterside or holiday homes. It creates a sense of informality, ease and flow, as well as optimizing the available light and space. Practical, hard-working kitchens extend into airy, unfussy living spaces that in turn lead onto broad terraces, deep porches or open decks. Where possible, the living space should occupy the best vantage point for appreciating the surrounding landscape. If you can insert or enlarge windows, ensure that they are as big as possible, to make the most of the views and the natural light. Remember that rooms facing east will be bright and light all morning long, so are ideal for kitchens and breakfast rooms, while those facing west will capture the rays of the evening sun.

Bedrooms are best kept simple and utilitarian, with uncarpeted floors, simple storage and built-in bunks in the children's rooms. Bathrooms should be practical and resilient, with powerful showers and easy-to-mop floors. Outdoor showers are always a useful addition, tucked away close to the pool or on the way back from the beach, while outdoor kitchens or food-preparation areas encourage long, laid-back, alfresco meals.

ABOVE: To maintain a sense of flow through the space, a 'floating' stair has been designed to obstruct as little of the room as possible.

OPPOSITE: Exposed beams and trusses open up a roof space and add a lofty sense of volume and scale. Combined with large expanses of glass on both sides of the room, the open roof ensures a light and airy environment. Open space not only makes everything appear larger but also creates a more relaxed vibe.

RIGHT: In a large open-plan space, you can create areas of intimacy by arranging furniture into distinct 'zones'. This divides the space without the need for walls or other barriers. In this beach house, the floor-to-ceiling windows optimize the sea views and natural light, providing seamless interaction between indoors and out.

designing for sun & shade

While we all crave light, warmth and sunshine, there are also times when shade is required.

Even the prettiest terrace is not inviting unless it includes a shaded area in which to retreat from the midday sun, while open decks should be designed to offer areas of both sun and shade.

Pergolas are ideal shade solutions for sunny spots. They consist of vertical posts that support a framework of cross beams or an open lattice. Vines, wisteria or other climbers can be trained to grow over the top in order to provide attractive dappled light below. Pergolas are usually built over outdoor eating areas or to offer some shade over an open terrace. Awnings, umbrellas and canopies are less permanent ways of providing shade on a deck or terrace. They do offer flexibility but also have to be erected and taken down, and require storage space when not in use.

ABOVE LEFT: A metal pergola covers an outdoor entertaining area. Leafy wisteria is starting to scramble over it, providing a soft, dappled lighting effect and protecting diners from direct sunlight.

ABOVE CENTRE: Simple, roll-up willow blinds have been fitted externally over these French doors to keep out the harsh midday sun. They can be used when the doors are either open or shut.

ABOVE RIGHT: A large terrace is covered by a wooden pergola, which breaks up direct sunlight. Grapevines are being trained to cover it and will eventually provide a leafy ceiling to the outdoor room.

OPPOSITE: A slatted roof over the outdoor areas was incorporated into the design of this expansive deck, providing decorative shadow effects and a perfect balance of sun and shade.

porches & verandahs

Porches and verandahs are distinguishable from decks and terraces in that they are covered over or closed in.

Enclosed porches are a great addition to a summerhouse or waterside home as they allow for use all year round, offering warmth and comfort while still providing a sense of being outside.

A porch must be a versatile area – somewhere to entertain, eat meals and curl up and read, as well as a place to shed sandy shoes and wetsuits on the way back from the beach. Verandahs fulfil the same functions but are open at the sides with overhanging roofs to offer protection from the elements, thus increasing the amount of time that people can spend in the open air.

ABOVE: The lush pot plants create a feeling that the house is extending into the garden, or vice versa.

OPPOSITE ABOVE LEFT: A completely enclosed porch is flooded with natural light. The internal windows allow light to penetrate to the main section of the house.

OPPOSITE ABOVE RIGHT: Sturdy canvas blinds are hung around this porch to provide protection from rain and shade from bright sunlight.

OPPOSITE BELOW LEFT: A deep porch such as this one can be used all day long and all year round. It offers a cool retreat from the hot sun as well as shelter from the rain.

OPPOSITE BELOW RIGHT: This porch acts as an outdoor room for relaxation and entertainment. It is furnished with a plump sofa and a rocking chair, but the oversized planting gives occupants the impression of being outdoors.

decks & terraces

No house by the water would be complete without a deck or a terrace. They provide an essential connection or bridge between the point of shelter – the house – and the greater landscape, as well as giving an excellent vantage point from which to appreciate the natural beauty of the surroundings.

A terrace is generally a paved or tiled area, whereas a deck is a wooden structure, often raised. Both are outdoor living spaces, where entertaining, eating and socializing take place in the open air. When designing or refurbishing a waterside home, plan the largest possible glass doors or French windows onto the terrace or deck, to blur the boundaries between inside and out.

LEFT: A large deck runs alongside the internal living space of this beach house giving glorious views of the ocean. Partially covered to provide both sun and shade, it can be used even on the hottest summer days.

OPPOSITE ABOVE LEFT: Sturdy stone pillars support a pergola over this terrace. As the vines grow, their foliage will provide some cover overhead.

OPPOSITE ABOVE RIGHT: A small deck is an idyllic setting from which to survey the distant sea.

OPPOSITE BELOW LEFT: This deck becomes a verandah along the side of the house, providing outdoor areas for all weather conditions.

OPPOSITE BELOW RIGHT: Even the smallest terrace can offer a relaxed area for outdoor entertaining.

windows

Windows in all shapes, sizes and styles are crucial elements of a waterside home, since they frame those all-important views.

Advances in glass technology have led to the creation of huge panoramic windows that allow the view to become the focal point of a room. In more traditional houses, the aim is to keep the windows as bare as possible, to optimize the views and allow natural light to flood in.

If some sort of window covering is preferred, the options include simple fabric or natural-fibre blinds/shades, plantation-style shutters or floaty drapes. External shutters provide additional security and protection from the elements, and control the amount of sunlight that enters.

OPPOSITE ABOVE LEFT: Plantation-style shutters work well in rooms that receive direct sunlight. They can be manually adjusted so that the light levels can be controlled.

OPPOSITE ABOVE RIGHT: A pair of arched windows frames a leafy garden view. They are hinged so that they open like French doors.

OPPOSITE BELOW: Windows line two sides of this all-white bedroom, creating a cool, breezy interior.

BELOW LEFT: Salvaged French windows have been cleverly converted into doors. Within each panel is a smaller window that can be opened independently when the main doors are closed.

BELOW: This guest room doesn't overlook the sea, but the clever placing of the wide barn-style windows mean that it still includes views over the water – in this case, over the swimming pool.

MATERIALS
& TEXTURES

wood

Whether old or new, polished or painted or simply left untreated to age naturally, wood has a timeless beauty.

Natural materials are obvious choices for a waterside home and wood works hard both inside and out. It weathers well in coastal climates, with salty air and sunlight bleaching it to a silver-grey hue. Wooden shingles are often chosen for exteriors, as they are low maintenance and able to endure harsh coastal weather conditions.

Wood also has a role to play in interior spaces, where walls, floors and ceilings are often clad with wood and painted – with either a single coat of emulsion/latex that allows the grain to show through or a high gloss that reflects natural light.

OPPOSITE ABOVE LEFT: White-painted boards in a variety of widths line a corridor. This inexpensive solution makes a great visual impact.

OPPOSITE ABOVE RIGHT: A combination of reclaimed wood and painted boards, laid both vertically and horizontally, creates an interesting layered effect.

OPPOSITE BELOW LEFT: Cypress wood gives a strong, linear feel to the exterior of this beachfront home.

OPPOSITE BELOW RIGHT: The rich hues of natural wood bring warmth and intimacy to all-white interiors.

ABOVE LEFT: Walls, floors and ceilings are all clad with wooden boards and painted glossy white and pale grey for a summery feel.

ABOVE: Old wooden shelving from a porcelain factory was used to make this flooring. Faint circles of clay from where the pots once dried remain visible to this day.

stone, concrete & tiles

Hard surfaces, such as stone and concrete, are versatile and durable materials for floors, walls, countertops and fireplace surrounds in coastal interiors.

Rough stone walls bring a pleasingly rugged touch to a relaxed waterside home, and while a whitewashed, plastered finish can be beautifully simple, partially exposed stonework, as in Isabel López-Quesada's home (see pages 94–107), can create a striking focal point in a room.

Cool and smooth to the touch, concrete flooring is compatible with radiant underfloor heating, making it is pleasant to walk on in any season. It comes in a variety of colours and can be polished or waxed for a smooth, sleek finish. Ceramic or terracotta tiles are also widely used in the houses featured in this book and provide a practical surface that is particularly appropriate in warmer climates.

ABOVE LEFT: A fireplace surround is constructed of natural stone stacked to give the appearance of a structural stone wall.

ABOVE CENTRE: Slate that originally formed part of oyster beds has been cleverly reused as flooring, laid in a parquetry pattern on a large outdoor terrace.

ABOVE RIGHT: Reclaimed terracotta ceiling tiles have been used to make a stunning entrance floor.

OPPOSITE: Hexagonal tiles surrounded by poured concrete create an unusual inlaid effect on this bathroom floor. The design was actually an ingenious solution, as the owner fell in love with the antique tiles but did not have enough to cover the entire floor.

glass & metal

Glass is a ubiquitous feature of houses in waterfront locations, for it not only ensures that rooms are flooded with the luminescent coastal light, but also allows the occupants to make the most of wonderful coastal views.

In many of the houses in this book, glass is used extensively. Large expanses of glass in the form of picture windows and sliding doors tend to create a cool, contemporary feel, whereas smaller windows and French doors have more traditional charm.

Copper, brass and stainless steel are hardy metals that are rust resistant and can stand up well to the salt-laden air in coastal areas. Copper is a popular choice for roofing thanks to the attractive verdigris patina it develops with age.

OPPOSITE ABOVE LEFT: Corrugated tin, salvaged and patchworked together on the walls, is an unexpected choice for a waterside home.

OPPOSITE ABOVE RIGHT: Floor-to-ceiling frameless glass brings the surrounding landscape in.

OPPOSITE BELOW: Metal-framed windows open onto an outdoor space where a powder-coated metal pergola echoes the strong right angles of the main building.

BELOW LEFT: Large expanses of glass framed in unobtrusive metal surrounds allow this living space to benefit from uninterrupted views and an abundance of natural light.

BELOW RIGHT: Floor-to-ceiling glass panels form a covered walkway that links two separate areas of this house. The frameless installation also makes the passage appear to be open to the elements.

linen, cotton, & rattan

Resilient, hardwearing and a pleasure to touch, natural materials are the ideal choice for homes with easy waterside style.

When it comes to textiles, nubbly linen is perfect and well suited to warm climates, as it is cool and breathes easily. Linen sits harmoniously alongside other natural textures and materials, particularly rustic wood and unpolished stone.

Cotton is another good choice. In a coastal abode, utilitarian white cotton canvas slipcovers are washable and hard wearing, while floaty, loosely woven muslin is often used for mosquito nets. Cotton ticking also works well – its jaunty stripes give it a casual seaside feel, and the tight weave makes it ideal for mattresses and cushions.

Another natural material that adds visual interest to a coastal home is rattan, which is used to make wicker and cane furniture. Its intricate weave introduces texture and an air of informal chic.

ABOVE LEFT: This heavily textured, coarsely woven linen throw with a long, trailing fringe offers an intriguing tactile contrast to a woven rope chair.

ABOVE CENTRE: The warm hue of natural wicker is often a welcome addition to light and airy seaside decorating schemes. Wicker planters make perfect containers for pretty flowering plants and are a quick and easy way to add a bit of textural contrast to a room.

ABOVE: The woven seat and back of this mid-century classic – the Hans Wegner CH-25 lounge chair – looks like rattan but is actually made from paper cord. Despite its iconic status, the chair has a relaxed feel that works well in a beach house.

OPPOSITE: A wicker sofa has a plump seat pad covered in white cotton. Colour and interest is added by the layers of cushions in florals and checks, which create a cosy, informal effect.

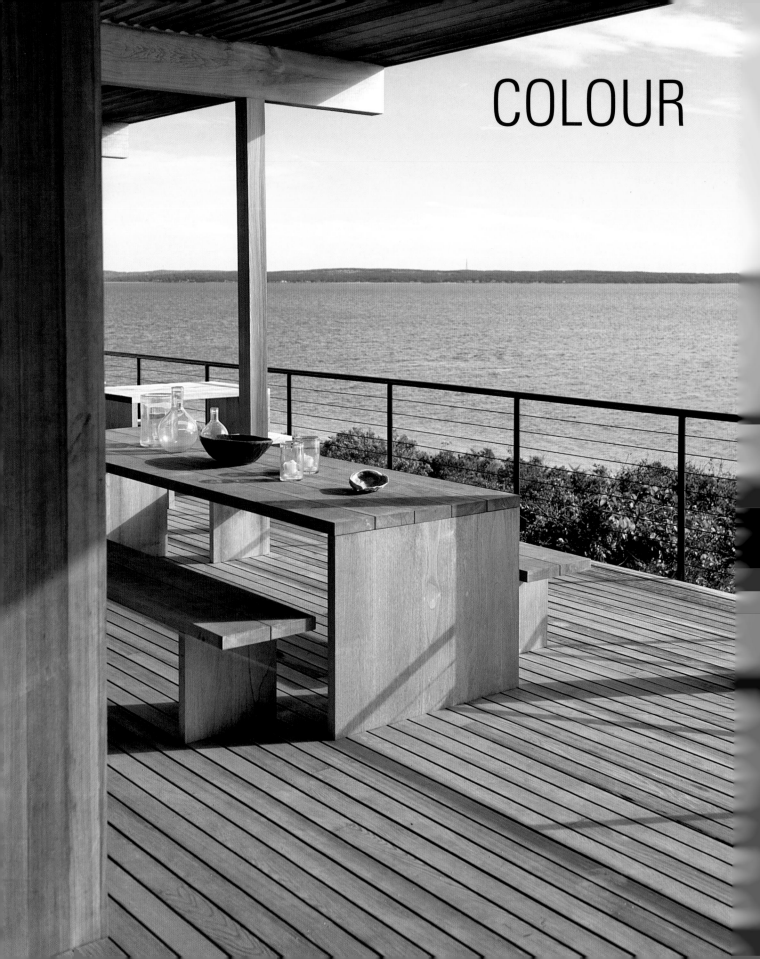

COLOUR

watery hues

Calming shades that reflect the ocean are often incorporated into coastal colour schemes to capture the sense of tranquillity and harmony that we associate with being close to water.

Large stretches of water reflect the colours of the sky and provide a broad palette to inspire interior decoration. Opt for tones ranging from muted blues through to soft greens and subtle turquoises, which bring to mind the sparkle of sun on water and wide, cloudless horizons.

Greys also work well in a coastal interior scheme, reminiscent as they are of windswept water and stormy skies. Greys are either warm or cool in tone – the cooler hues work beautifully with pale aquas and sea greens, while warmer shades can complement stronger colours such as navy, terracotta and brown.

Whichever you choose, these soothing watery hues will provide a restful backdrop for easy and relaxing coastal living.

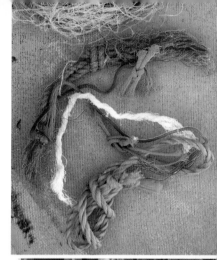

OPPOSITE: The ever-changing colours of sea and sky provide a huge spectrum from which to choose a suitable scheme.

ABOVE RIGHT: The faded blues and greens of fishermen's rope washed up on shore spark ideas for coastal interiors.

RIGHT: The strong cerulean blue of this vintage cabinet sings out within a neutral decorative scheme.

BELOW LEFT: A vibrant blue linoleum floor makes reference to the water that surrounds this island dwelling.

BELOW: Old glass bottles and nautical floats are grouped together to reflect a myriad of translucent ocean hues.

moody tones

The natural palette of stones, pebbles, shells, beach grass and sand is a great source of inspiration for coastal colour schemes.

Rich browns, golden yellows and sage greens make for atmospheric, dramatic interiors. While nautical blues and cools whites are frequently associated with seaside living, these warmer, deeper colours offer a refreshing alternative.

Neutral beach tones, on the other hand, take their cue from sun-bleached driftwood, sandy shores and faded beach grass and make for restful interiors. And a neutral scheme offers an opportunity to introduce the odd splash of bold colour, such as deep turquoise or coral pink.

ABOVE: In this room, the original wooden walls are the perfect backdrop for a colour scheme inspired by grasses, sand, sun and shells. Browns, subtle golds and mossy greens, spiked with the odd splash of white, create an intimate, luxurious effect.

OPPOSITE ABOVE LEFT: Crisp white linens lighten and add contrast to a timber-clad room.

OPPOSITE ABOVE AND BELOW RIGHT: Cedar wood that is left to weather develops shades of silver and charcoal, while cedar that has not been exposed to sunlight and rain retains its rich reddish hue.

OPPOSITE BELOW LEFT: A rugged landscape of windswept grasses and pine trees with sea and sky beyond represents a colour chart inspired by nature.

harmonious whites

An all-white interior is an obvious choice for a waterside home because it creates a cool, crisp and airy environment, as well as providing a blank canvas against which to display collections of marine treasures.

Bright whites are good in hot climates as they reflect light and make things feel cool. Warmer whites and creamy tones work wonderfully in cooler climates, as they have more depth.

A predominantly white space will also give the appearance of being larger and brighter than it actually is, so where space is limited consider white as a starting point upon which to build and layer other subtle tones.

White doesn't have to mean stark and cold. Combine it with natural materials such as wood, linen, coir and seagrass – their sun-bleached tones suggest a summery, beachy palette and are well suited to the relaxed simplicity of waterside living.

OPPOSITE: A large sandy-coloured coir rug completes a natural beach palette in this all-white living room – gloss-painted walls and floors, wooden Venetian blinds and cotton canvas upholstery all combine to create a invitingly relaxed effect.

ABOVE LEFT: Natural wood, in the form of well-placed furniture, softens this airy all-white corridor. The smooth concrete floors are a creamier hue, warming up the pristine walls and the large artwork.

ABOVE CENTRE: Exposed wooden beams, wooden furniture and woven accessories breathe life into a predominantly white interior.

ABOVE: White grounded with accents of slate grey and charcoal makes for a simple, monochromatic scheme. Washable slipcovers such as these are perfect for an all-white scheme because they can be tossed into the washing machine when they start to look a little dingy and emerge spotlessly clean.

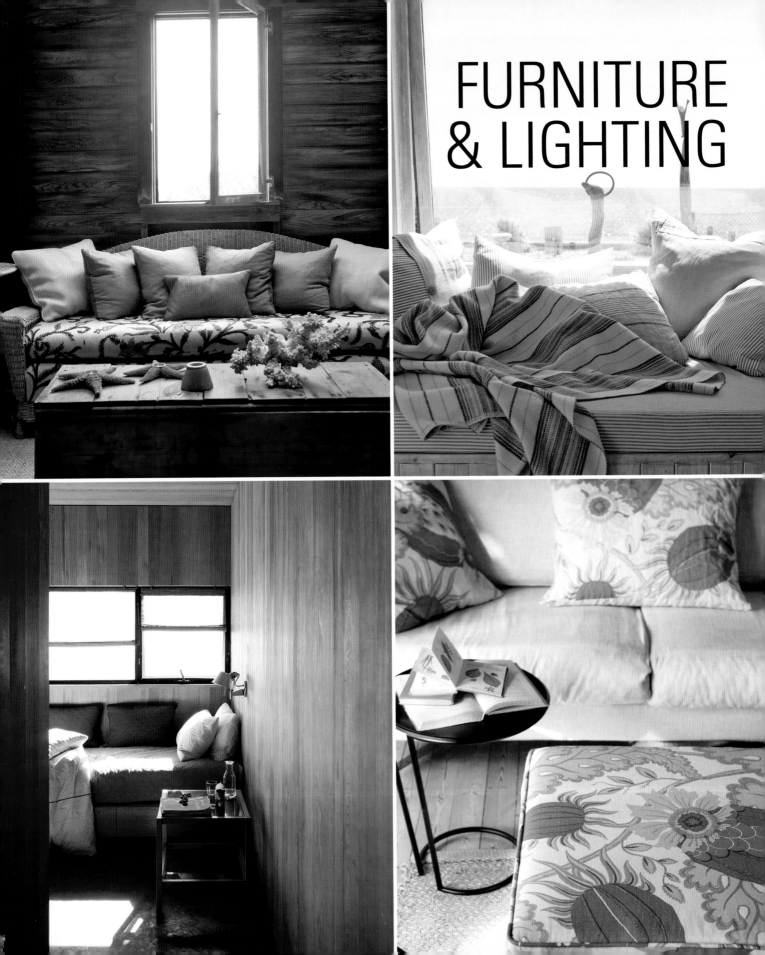

FURNITURE
& LIGHTING

daybeds, sofas & comfy chairs

Comfortable furniture is an important aspect of summer living. Since relaxation is high on the agenda, seating should be abundant and carefully positioned.

Daybeds are perfectly suited to a waterside dwelling and can be custom built into a room with a view. Chaises longues add a note of elegance, as do vintage French metal examples dressed with plump bolsters and cushions. Slipcovers are the ideal upholstery solution for sofas. Choose hardwearing fabric that is machine washable and will withstand the rigours of holiday lifestyles. Squashy sofas look inviting piled with cushions, which are also a good way to introduce colour and pattern into a simple, pared-down interior.

OPPOSITE ABOVE LEFT: A broad cane sofa is upholstered in vintage crewelwork and finished with cushions in an assortment of complementary colours.

OPPOSITE ABOVE RIGHT: This sun-drenched daybed has been built in below a sea-facing window.

OPPOSITE BELOW LEFT: Built-in beds double as seating during the day. They reflect the efficient nature of boat interiors.

OPPOSITE BELOW RIGHT: A simple white sofa complements a boldly patterned ottoman and accent cushions in the same fabric.

BELOW: Sofas and armchairs in rattan, wicker or cane introduce colour and texture into any room and look good on porches or verandahs. An assortment of scatter cushions makes this Colonial-style set of furniture particularly inviting.

beds & bedding

Seaside homes are designed for holiday time, during which their inhabitants spend most of the day out of doors and close to the water. Accordingly, coastal bedrooms need to be no more than comfortable and practical.

A variety of different beds are suitable – painted wood, four-posters and pretty wrought-iron bedsteads are all good choices, not to mention the ubiquitous bunks. Beds are ideal for showcasing beautiful fabrics. From crisp white cotton sheets to soft crumpled linens, opt for lots of dazzling white with accents of blue, the odd stripe or simple pattern. Place classic quilts and throws on the end of the bed so they are easy to reach during the night when cool sea breezes blow in.

OPPOSITE ABOVE: This bed is positioned to face the view through double doors that open directly onto a swimming pool. Crisp white bed linen is accented with colourful cushions, a neatly upholstered headboard and a tailored throw.

OPPOSITE BELOW LEFT: Vintage maritime accessories and boat prints are a reminder of the house's waterside location in this snug, welcoming guest bedroom.

OPPOSITE BELOW RIGHT: Bunk beds are a brilliant solution when space is limited. Children love them, and they are particularly practical when extra beds are required for guests.

BELOW: Simplicity, practicality and comfort reign in this all-white bedroom. Nothing is allowed to detract from the views. Large windows overlook the garden, while the French doors lead onto a balcony that overlooks the ocean.

outdoor furniture

There are endless styles and types of outdoor furniture to choose from, so select pieces that suit the location and the purpose.

Whether choosing comfortable seating for conversation and relaxation, tables and chairs for alfresco dining or sunbeds for the pool, make sure that any furniture to be used outside is durable and will stand up to all weather conditions.

Teak furniture is widely used in outdoor settings because it fades naturally and beautifully in sunlight. Metal and wrought-iron pieces, such as pretty daybeds and café-style tables and chairs, are also ideal for outdoor use and are both durable and elegant. Folding metal or wooden chairs are a good choice too, and don't take up too much room when packed away. Wicker and cane furniture feels at home in a coastal environment, and synthetic rattan is resistant to heat, light and moisture, so it can be left out all year round.

ABOVE LEFT: A pair of luxurious, double daybeds bring a hint of Riviera chic to this deep, shady terrace at a house outside Biarritz in south-west France. Their wicker bases are topped with contrastingly coloured upholstered mattresses.

ABOVE CENTRE: A woven cotton hammock is slung casually between two trees – the ideal place to while away a few hours with a good book in this idyllic rustic setting.

ABOVE RIGHT: Retro 1950s-style seating made of strung plastic and metal brings a sense of fun and nostalgia to this modern beach hut on the English coast. The hot orange shade adds a vivid blast of colour to the sun-bleached decking.

OPPOSITE: The clean, angular lines of this outdoor teak furniture is combined with crisply tailored white cotton canvas covers. The overall effect perfectly complements a minimalist deck setting on Long Island.

lighting

Natural light has a peculiarly luminescent quality by the coast, illuminating waterside homes with a wonderful glow.

Additional light sources should therefore be subtle, and a mixture of pendant, floor and table lamps will create practical and pleasing lighting effects. Both traditional and industrial-style metal light fittings are well suited to coastal homes, as are simple rustic pendants and shades.

Outdoor lighting must be durable and able to withstand the elements, so make sure that electrical fittings are designed for outdoor use and won't rust or deteriorate readily. Don't forget candlelight, whose evocative, atmospheric effects are ideal for long summer nights.

BELOW LEFT: A simple metal pendant light hangs low over a table, reflecting the clean lines of this modern kitchen.

BELOW RIGHT: Exterior wall-mounted fittings with an industrial edge, like this Belgian deck light, work well on porches and terraces.

OPPOSITE ABOVE LEFT: A quirky, one-off, twisted-wire light fitting creates a focal point and accentuates the high ceiling in a guest bedroom.

OPPOSITE ABOVE RIGHT: A single bulb suspended from a length of flex is perfectly in keeping with the deconstructed style of this interior.

OPPOSITE BELOW LEFT: A vintage Moroccan lantern has been wired up to the electricity supply to illuminate a shady terrace.

OPPOSITE BELOW RIGHT: Vintage-style lights hang over an outdoor dining table, while a large candelabrum takes centre stage.

COLLECTING
& DISPLAY

shells, stones & pebbles

Beautiful objects found washed up on the shore can be collected and put to decorative use in a multitude of simple and stylish ways.

Stones, shells and other natural treasures look striking when used to create displays, strung together to make hanging decorations or piled into glass jars, vases and hurricane lanterns.

Smooth grey pebbles or delicate shells need no additional embellishment – arrange them in a line running along windowsills and bookshelves, or cluster them together on tables and consoles. A collection of larger shells and corals can look wonderful displayed behind glass in a cabinet or vitrine, where their intricate forms and delicate hues can be admired in all their glory.

OPPOSITE ABOVE: Broken shells gathered on long beach walks have been gradually added to a wooden fence, making a decorative border.

OPPOSITE BELOW LEFT: Shells picked up from the beach at low tide create an elegant still life rich in colour and texture.

OPPOSITE BELOW RIGHT: Sea-smoothed pebbles make a minimal but effective centrepiece for a long wooden dining table.

BELOW LEFT: A hurricane lantern filled with pebbles or shells to hold a sturdy candle in place adds interest to a windowsill.

BELOW RIGHT: The owners of this Danish coastal cabin collected pebbles with holes in them and strung them together to hang like wind chimes. Paired with a frond of dried seaweed and a piece of driftwood, they make a simple but intriguing display.

maps, objects, & pictures

The pieces we choose to put on display are an expression of our individual taste and style. In a beach house or holiday home, it seems fitting to choose items that are relevant to the surroundings and the activities enjoyed there.

Sun hats, vintage tennis racquets, wooden oars and other beach paraphernalia can all be collected and displayed as decorative elements in a coastal environment. Maps or navigation charts are popular adornments and look good either framed or attached directly to the wall, particularly if they are old and worn. Nostalgic postcards have a similar effect. Nautical artwork has a place too, especially vintage examples. Grouped together, artworks can create a dramatic effect on a wall.

BELOW LEFT: Straw hats and bags casually displayed on the wall are conveniently on hand for visits to the beach.

BELOW RIGHT: A collection of vintage fans finds a perfect home in an enclosed entrance porch.

OPPOSITE ABOVE LEFT: Vintage maps make great wall art, particularly if they reference local geography. This map of France has found its proper place in a Biarritz kitchen.

OPPOSITE ABOVE RIGHT: Wildlife etchings hang in homemade frames on a painted pine wall.

OPPOSITE BELOW LEFT: White American pottery is arranged in a cluster of pleasingly organic shapes and sizes.

OPPOSITE BELOW RIGHT: Botanic prints of fungi are framed identically in simple wooden frames and hung in an ordered grid to create a graphic display on a white wall.

PART 2

Homes

OPPOSITE: A central covered breezeway overlooking the beach defines the entry, and is accessed by both front and rear staircases. It also divides the living spaces and bedrooms. The cypress wood cladding has weathered to a faded silver colour. A slatted roof provides a combination of sun and shade.

RIGHT AND BELOW: The building is cantilevered on one side to create a shaded carport. This also provides beach access from the front of the house, via a secluded pathway through the dunes.

FAR RIGHT: Hovering just above the dunes, the top floor and deck have uninterrupted views of sand and water. The private beach is only a few steps from the house.

WATER'S EDGE

The first impression of this Shelter Island house is its proximity to the water. Upon climbing the front stairs to the large, covered breezeway that forms the entrance to the house, a panoramic view of beach, water and horizon greets the visitor. This striking open space gives an immediate understanding of the connection between the house and the ocean in front of it.

Located in a quiet pocket of this charming island, the site was originally occupied by a single-storey, 1960s shack that was virtually uninhabitable by the time the current owner, architect Cary Tamarkin, bought it. However, the Tamarkins lived there for three years while designing and obtaining building permits for the new house, which was helpful in understanding the character and perspectives of the plot.

ABOVE: Discreet wall hooks directly inside the front door provide a simple storage solution for sunhats, bags and beach towels.

ABOVE RIGHT: Cedar wood lines the interior walls and ceilings, while concrete is used for floors, kitchen counters and the fireplace surround.

OPPOSITE: The open-plan kitchen, dining and living space has floor-to-ceiling windows and doors leading to the large deck overlooking the beach. A variety of seating areas break up the space without enclosing it. Hans Wegner chairs create an area for conversation around the fireplace.

They enjoyed this time and wanted to retain the sense of informality that came from the original structure, while capitalizing on its closeness to the glorious stretch of private beach below.

Cary Tamarkin's aim was to create a holiday home to accommodate a family of four plus ample space for guests. The covered breezeway not only acts as a striking entrance but also separates the living spaces from the bedrooms on the top storey of the house, thus dividing public and private areas to encourage a casual holiday atmosphere. On the lower level are more bedrooms, a bathroom and a utility room, all of which can be accessed externally from the beach side of the building, creating a self-contained guest area that is still very much part of the house.

The outdoor spaces are the most important aspects in the design, as the family spend the majority of their time outside during the summer months. The main deck runs the whole length of the living space, with wide-open views on one side and floor-to-ceiling glass doors and windows on the other.

On the main deck, a combination of custom-designed teak furniture and simple cream upholstery provides a luxurious setting for relaxing and socializing. The deck railing is made from painted stainless-steel tubing with marine cable inserts to enable maximum transparency while still meeting building regulations. This large deck is where most activities take place, with the beach just a few steps away via the rear staircase.

ABOVE: The clean-lined teak dining tables and bench seats on the main deck are arranged with linear precision, appearing almost as part of the deck itself.

LEFT: The house's private jetty 'floats' in the ocean at high tide.

There is ample space here for relaxing, sociable conversing, solitary reading and family dinners, with various seating and lounging areas to choose from depending on the activity at hand. There is also another small deck just off the master bedroom, complete with an outdoor shower that faces the sea – an idyllic place to rinse off after early morning or evening swims.

The deck areas are covered spaces, although they do not feel enclosed. The 'ceilings' are formed by the deep roof overhang, which has pierced openings to admit partial sunlight, resulting in a mixture of sun and shade. This practical solution also provides a graphic display of light and shadow that constantly changes as the sun moves from east to west overhead. The outdoor furniture was custom designed and is made of teak, which has weathered to the same silver shade as the rest of the house. The clean lines and square angles of its design create an illusion that it is part of the deck itself.

The interior and exterior walls and exposed structural elements are constructed from responsibly harvested cypress wood, left untreated so it will fade to silver over time. This is an excellent natural material for waterfront locations, as it is extremely robust and rot-resistant. Floors are concrete, with radiant heating beneath for the cooler months of the year. Wood and concrete are the main finishes used both inside and out, the architect preferring to work with a limited palette of materials.

The living space is open plan and easy to navigate. A neat kitchen and dining space sit immediately inside the main entrance, with floor-to-ceiling windows running the whole length of the space and optimizing the amazing sea views. There is an informal seating area in front of a simple fireplace, and a comfortable lounge with a study tucked away behind it at the far end. The entire space is one long, open room that offers uninterrupted lines of sight out over the ocean and is flooded from dawn to dusk with natural light.

Every bedroom is built on the ocean side of the house, within earshot of the waves – a calming and soothing way to wake up or to drift off to sleep. Most of the furniture is built in, including the beds – quite possibly influenced by the efficient nature of boat interiors, although this wasn't a conscious decision. The limited amount of freestanding furniture is a mix of styles, much of it mid-twentieth century. The architecture of this period also had an influence on how the house was designed.

ABOVE: Inside and outside become one with floor-to-ceiling windows that optimize the view and keep interior spaces light and bright. A walnut-topped Eero Saarinen Tulip table is surrounded by Hans Wegner dining chairs from Cary Tamarkin's collection of fine twentieth-century furniture.

ABOVE: All the bedrooms are on the ocean side of the house, so their occupants are lulled to sleep by the sound of the waves breaking on the shore. Built-in beds double as seating in the children's rooms and have a boat-like feel, keeping everything tidy and shipshape.

ABOVE RIGHT: The tranquil master bedroom looks out onto a small deck complete with outdoor shower (opposite) and is bathed in light right through the day.

The cypress wood used throughout the house led interior designer Suzanne Shaker to combine warm colours and natural fibres when selecting the furnishings. She was also inspired by the way of life and natural beauty that surrounds and supports island living. The interior is spare and considered, with built-in cabinetry enabling a well-organized, clutter-free environment. Lighting was kept to a minimum so as not to overpower the night sky. Paper lamps by Japanese American artist Isamu Noguchi, and other discreet task lighting enhance the subtle gleam of the cypress wood.

In addition to the front entrance stairs, there is also easy access to the house from the beach side via a separate staircase leading up to the main deck. This second staircase also links the guest rooms downstairs with the main living areas above.

The proximity of the private beach is undoubtedly one of the house's finest assets. Since sunbathing and socializing mostly takes place on the deck, Cary was keen to keep the beach free and open, and two sun-bleached Adirondack chairs and a table are the only pieces of furniture here. The landscape has been left almost untouched, so the house appears to have been dropped whole onto a large dune.

From a distance, this house looks as if it hovers gently above the sand dunes and beach vegetation. Elevating it slightly in this way takes full advantage of the constant breeze from the south-west and allows sweeping views of the beach and sunsets. Exquisite locations such as this are greatly sought after, yet increasingly rare. The beach, for these lucky owners, is quite literally their back yard.

ABOVE LEFT: A skylight in the en-suite bathroom floods the shower space with natural light and gives a feeling of being outdoors.

ABOVE: The small deck that leads off the master bedroom was designed within the rectangular footprint of the house and is open to the sky above and the ocean in front.

OPPOSITE: Floor-to-ceiling windows frame a view of the ocean. They are also a clever solution to the problem of how to optimize the outlook, given tight restrictions as to where and how the house could be positioned on the land.

RIGHT: The nearby beach provides inspiration in terms of colours and textures.

FAR RIGHT: Windows were deliberately placed at a low height so that sea views can be enjoyed even from the outdoor area at the rear of the house.

DANISH DAYDREAMS

Denmark has its own distinct design heritage, yet Danish architects Hanne Dalsgaard and Henrik Jeppesen's summer house is inspired by concepts and materials from distant corners of the globe. Living areas reflect the Japanese custom of welcoming nature into the house, whereas the exterior timber comes from the far-flung cedar forests of Canada.

When Hanne and Henrik bought the empty plot, it was effectively a small patch of land covered with trees and shrubs and offering occasional glimpses of the nearby ocean. For the first three summers they stayed on site in an old caravan and lived primitively, using an outdoor kitchen and cold water. They wanted to discover exactly what the land could give them – where the sun came up and where it set, where the best views were, and the direction of the wind and rain.

It transpired that the couple could build on only one side of the site because of historic planning restrictions, so the house had to be narrow.

ABOVE: The exterior is clad in cedar wood, which has a strong, distinctive grain and weathers to a silver shade. It is naturally durable and thus ideal for coastal locations.

The living area is one big room, purposely designed for ease of living. Interior spaces have been kept simple in terms of both colour and design to allow the landscape to take centre stage. The owners wanted a connection between inside and out, hence the porch that runs the length of the building.

ABOVE: Built along one wall, the kitchen is of simple construction. Open shelving above and below the countertop keeps everything within easy reach.

ABOVE RIGHT: A day bed is built into a nook in the living room and doubles as a spare bed for guests. It is an inviting spot in which to curl up and read on rainy days.

OPPOSITE ABOVE: The bedrooms have a cabin-like feel. Both have built-in bunks with striped ticking covers for a relaxed, summery feel.

OPPOSITE BELOW: Large double doors open from the main bedroom onto the deck. The white-painted interior is a contrast to the naturally weathered, cedar-clad exterior.

Hanne and Henrik wanted to capture as much of the ocean view as possible, and clearing the land to accommodate the building also left a beautiful outlook across the wooded terrain. With forest on one side and the sound and sight of the ocean on the other, they were able to optimize the views from the house and plan the interior spaces accordingly.

A connection to nature is at the heart of the design, and the interplay between indoors and out is emphasized with a neutral interior palette, especially chosen to highlight the brighter natural colours found in the surrounding landscape – a concept gleaned from the couple's numerous trips to Japan and fascination with Japanese architectural concepts. It was important that the house was calm and tranquil, and the flow of the rooms combines with a soft and subtle colour scheme to achieve such an environment.

The spatial arrangements have been cleverly considered so that the two bedrooms form 'cabins' at each end of the house with the main living area sandwiched between them. The main bedroom and bathroom can be closed off completely for privacy and are separated from the rest of the house by an entrance portal with large sliding doors on either side. This is the main access point for the house as well as a space to discard beach shoes and watersports equipment in summer and muddy boots in winter.

The kitchen and living area is one big open-plan space, purposely designed for practicality. Floor-to-ceiling windows frame a stunning view to the ocean beyond the exposed terrace at the front, and French doors open onto the covered porch that runs the length of the house and connects inside and out. A large day bed is built into one side of the space, providing a place to relax during the day as well as additional accommodation for guests. A casual seating area is positioned perfectly to take advantage of the view. Over the years, Hanne has scoured flea markets and junk shops for rattan chairs from the 1950s and dresses up her finds with new cushions.

Interior spaces have been kept simple in terms of both colour and design. Walls are tongue-and-groove pine painted white and the wooden floors have a linseed-oil finish. The nearby beach provides inspiration for the tones and textures of the decor. The kitchen cabinets are basic pine structures with open shelves both above and below, piled high with china, utensils and glassware. In the bedrooms, built-in bunk beds are covered with cosy duvets in crisp white or blue-striped ticking.

ABOVE: Thanks to strategically placed windows, the sea is visible from the outdoor food prep area at the back of the house.

OPPOSITE ABOVE: Wooden decking wraps around the exterior. Some sections are covered to offer shade and protection from the rain, others left open to capture sunshine.

OPPOSITE BELOW: The central entranceway can be completely closed off by large, barn-style sliding doors on each side.

To get the most enjoyment from the Danish summer, the house boasts numerous outdoor spaces and areas that can be used in all climactic conditions. The weather, as well as the time of the day, determines where the family spend their time. A deep porch wraps around the front and side of the house, and the rear terrace is sheltered from cold winds and ocean breezes. This is where the family tend to eat, and it is equipped with a practical outdoor kitchen area complete with a sink for preparing food. In order to make the most of the view, Hanne and Henrik designed a series of small windows at seating height that look through the open-plan interior space and frame views to the ocean beyond.

The exterior of the house is clad in Canadian cedar, which was given to them by a former client. It is an unusual material for summerhouses in this area, but the wood weathers well, has natural resistance to rot and decay,

and is very low maintenance. Over the years, the cedar has weathered to a rich palette of faded red, bleached silver and charcoal.

Found objects such as rocks, twigs and driftwood from the beach make instant works of art and adds personal touches both inside and out. Beach stones have been loosely strung together and hung on the roughly painted white walls. Shells picked up from the shore have been framed or artfully arranged on windowsills and tables. Wild flowers gathered from the surrounding landscape are arranged loosely in simple china vases and jugs.

This Danish beachside house is one of great simplicity and beauty and achieves everything that its owners hoped for. It enjoys uninterrupted views of ocean, beach and forest, enables the occupants to spend the majority of their time outside, and brings family and friends together in a relaxed and inviting atmosphere.

OPPOSITE ABOVE LEFT: The shingle beach is accessed directly from the property and stretches as far as the eye can see.

OPPOSITE ABOVE RIGHT: Bright orange Sun chairs by Thomas Bramwell Design add a burst of colour to the weathered pine decking.

OPPOSITE BELOW: Double doors provide a large, open entry to the pavilion, creating an area where summer activities can take place both inside and out. The deck appears to float above the shingled border.

RIGHT: Simple steps lead to a decked pathway that accesses the beach. The shingle border around the lawn visually connects garden to beach.

ABOVE RIGHT: Driftwood fish add a decorative element to the exterior walls.

With sweeping views across the Channel to the Isle of Wight, this is an English summerhouse in the traditional sense. A small, roofed building in the grounds of a larger one, it was built as a place of retreat and relaxation, as well as to provide an additional space for its owner to use for entertaining during the summer months.

BEACH HUT HAVEN

When fashion and advertising photographer Crena Watson left London for Bracklesham Bay in England's West Sussex, her destination was a house that had once belonged to a dear friend, the celebrated photographer Robert Carlos Clarke. Situated right on the seafront, it became Crena's home as well as her workplace. Shortly after moving in, she decided she needed an extra room, something close to the sea and away from the house. This was to be primarily a thinking space, one designed for peace, escape and contemplation, with no clutter or evidence of her working life, which takes place in her studio on the other side of the house.

And so evolved her summerhouse, a detached, weathered-pine, flat-roofed pavilion on a floating deck at the end of her garden, just steps from the shingle beach. A deep border of pebbles surrounds and encloses the structure and echoes the shingle of the beach. Set amongst

ABOVE: The focal point of the room is a large daybed that has a painted tongue-and-groove base and is built in below a wide window that faces the ocean. A plump mattress plus a generous array of cushions and bolsters make it an inviting place from which to observe the beachscape beyond.

these stones is a curious display of driftwood sculptures, left by Clarke, who built them from wood that he found washed up on the beach, adding further charm to this idyllic seafront location.

The structure, which pays homage to the traditional English beach hut, has floor-to-ceiling glass entrance doors that open up like a large picture book. The adjoining decked area leads onto the small lawn, which serves as an entertaining and sunbathing space that really comes into its own on warm beach days.

Three wooden steps rise to weathered gates that open onto a small deck leading to the beach itself. The gates are rather whimsical; without fencing on either side they serve no real purpose in terms of privacy or security. They do, however, visually delineate private property from public beach

space without blocking the view or disturbing the charming sense of informality that this open area holds.

Inside, a large window faces the water and frames the ever-changing view, offering up a different seascape on each visit. Below it is a deep, custom-built daybed, furnished with a plump mattress and comfy cushions covered in vintage ticking. This is an inviting place to read, sleep and dream. Apart from the daybed, the only other furniture is a low-slung reading chair, a console table for books, magazines and lanterns, and a shelf to display artwork and treasures. Folding chairs can be carried outside when the weather is good, and the only appliance is a vintage-style radio.

Bright orange plastic and metal outdoor chairs adorn the decked area and add a splash of vibrant colour that contrasts with the beautifully

ABOVE: The previous owner of the house, photographer Robert Carlos Clarke, created this collection of curious sculptures from driftwood that was washed up on the beach. The landscaping is entirely sympathetic to the summerhouse's seaside location.

BELOW: A comfortable wood and rattan reading chair has a similar 1950s retro feel to the outdoor furniture. A vintage navigational chart hangs casually on the wall – a nod to the summerhouse's waterside location.

BELOW RIGHT: Books, magazines and art, as well as shells and rocks picked up from the beach, invite closer inspection on a white-painted console table.

weathered pine used for the exterior and decking. Although a contemporary design, they are indicative of Crena's retro style and love of 1950 furniture.

Since Crena wanted something that could be used in all weather conditions, she made sure that the summerhouse was well insulated. As a result, with its clear lines of sight and proximity to the ocean, the building keeps the weather at arm's length while embracing the view. Equally well suited to cosy winter use and socializing in the sunshine, this much-loved space perfectly illustrates the lifestyle benefits that even the simplest expansion can provide.

LEFT: The deck wraps around the pavilion and links it to the main house, ensuring ample outdoor space for entertaining and socializing. The Sun chairs provide a strong, graphic element.

OPPOSITE: The living area is open on both sides to optimize natural light, sunshine, views and breezes. Floor-to-ceiling retractable glass doors create a horizontal opening across the space, allowing the sun to flood in from the south and bounce off the ceiling towards the northern aspect that faces the lake.

ABOVE RIGHT: The entrance to the main house illustrates a harmonious combination of traditional elements and simple, modern design. Gabled roof lines and cedar shingles work well with right angles and glass panels.

RIGHT: The perfect place to relax: teak steamer chairs on the guest-house deck are positioned to take in views of both the lake and the swimming pool.

Situated in Montauk, the famous fishing and surfing town perched at the tip of New York State's Long Island, this lakefront home is what architect Robert Young refers to as a 'hybrid' – it has elements of a traditional design crossed with clean, modern lines.

ROOMS WITH A VIEW

The three elements of this home are carefully integrated, using materials that are common to the area. Cedar shingles, gabled roofs and white-painted woodwork give a barn-like feel to the buildings, while large expanses of floor-to-ceiling glass, exposed trusses and steel introduce a contemporary twist.

The brief the owners gave their architect was to create a house that would accommodate a growing family and close friends. They also wanted to make the most of the marvellous water views to the north, as well as the southern sun and breezes. The challenge was to design and position buildings on the site to maximize both.

The compound is made up of three separate buildings with distinct uses: the main house, the guest house – which doubles as a pool house – and the garage. The overall architectural style remains consistent, and each of the buildings is based on the concept of one large central space

that is open to both the north and south. Occupants can enjoy the views on the north side, while sunlight and breezes from the south can penetrate through to the other side of the space.

Architecturally, the main house is made up of three volumes – two smaller gabled structures bookend a central space that sits under an open gabled roof, running perpendicular to its two wings. This vast living area has an open-plan kitchen at one end and comfortable seating and a dining area at the other. The exposed structural trusses are painted white, creating a spacious, lofty effect. The floor-to-ceiling glass sliding doors on both northern and southern walls retract to create an open-sided room. The only subdivison here comes from the driftwood-clad partitions and storage elements that subtly demarcate the space.

This area is about relaxing, entertaining and sharing food with friends. Movements between the cooking and eating areas take place naturally and directly, and this simple but creative layout provides an opportunity for everyone in the room to have a sense of involvement with whatever is taking place. The large, L-shaped sofa is positioned to take in the view on one side

ABOVE AND OPPOSITE: The open-plan kitchen and living area is a wonderful space for communal cooking, eating, socializing and relaxing. An island unit enables casual interaction, with large industrial-style pendant lights overhead anchoring it in the space.

FAR LEFT AND LEFT: Solid wood-panelled structures, painted grey to resemble driftwood, house the built-in kitchen and frame the book shelves and storage unit. They also bring the room down to size and define the open space.

RIGHT: Curtains extend past the open shelving to close off the bedrooms from the living space on the other side. They have been used instead of doors to optimize the flow.

BELOW: The living and dining area benefits from large glass doors on either side which enable light to pour through the building.

and face the fireplace on the other. The kitchen area boasts a large island and open shelving for easy access.

At the far side of the house is a double storey containing bedrooms, a laundry room and a study. The upper floor is accessed by an open staircase with a sleek balustrade of steel cabling and yachting fixtures. While the bedrooms are separate, they are designed to maintain a sense of flow between one area and another, and curtains are used instead of doors to close them off. These are drawn neatly behind the built-in shelving unit of the living area when not in use, and also act as a screen for the open storage on the bedroom side.

The other gabled structure behind the kitchen houses the entrances and a guest bedroom. There are two arrival points to the house, the main one leading directly into the open living and kitchen space, and a 'mudroom' entrance, tucked in behind the beech hedge that runs along the front and back of the house. This access point has built-in seating and storage for boots, jackets and other all-weather paraphernalia, and is a containment area for sandy feet or wet clothing.

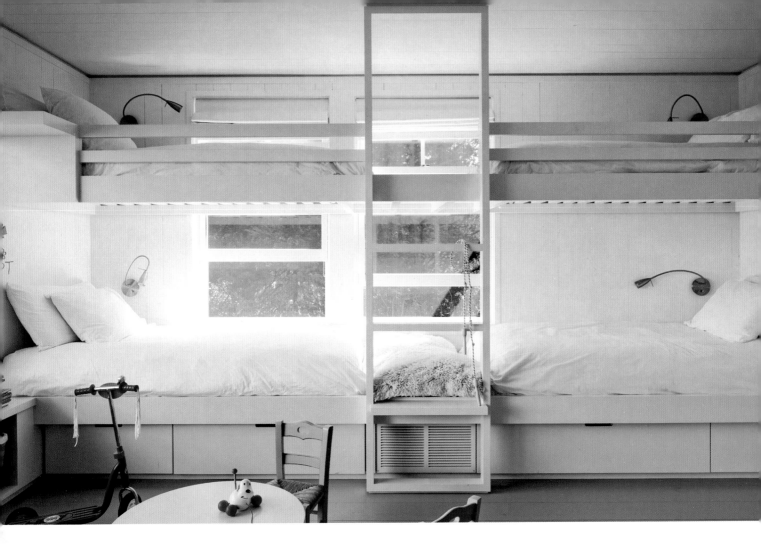

ABOVE: Custom-designed bunk beds in the children's room are built in. Large drawers underneath provide extra storage space and the ladder is fixed to both floor and ceiling for added stability.

OPPOSITE ABOVE: The view from the master bedroom takes in the garden and swimming pool, with the picturesque lake beyond.

OPPOSITE BELOW: The unspoilt shores of Lake Montauk, where the house is situated.

The interior spaces have been carefully designed to disguise the bulk of the building, as well as to create a variety of different views and experiences, highlighting points of interest in all directions. Large expanses of glass and white-painted wooden boarding form the walls, and the grey-painted pine floors and the tactile driftwood frame that surrounds the kitchen area the only items deviating from the otherwise entirely white palette. A child's vintage toy car in fire-engine red tucked away in a quiet corner and a collection of framed photographs with an ocean theme are the only notes of colour here.

It is no surprise that the detached guest house situated a short distance from the main house accommodates visitors in an equally stylish environment. Echoing the main house in many ways – it is open plan, with exposed trusses and lashings of white paint – it has its own small kitchen next to a long communal table with a mix of white vintage and brushed-metal Tolix chairs. A pair of bright red water skis make a bold display; the

single bolt of red amongst the monochromatic colour scheme is a subtle echo of the red of the vintage car that sits in the all-white interior of the main house.

This house doubles as a pool house in the summer months and has a wrap-around deck that faces the water. A few steps lower down is the immaculate garden and a 15-metre/50-foot lap pool, with edges so crisp and water so turquoise that even a brief glance makes one feel instantly refreshed.

The third of the structures – a barn-like garage – also opens up to the north and south, allowing vehicles and boats access to the private mooring on the lake at the end of the garden. Again, cedar shingles have been used here, giving a natural, weathered effect and offering a contrast to the white-painted sliding barn doors and window frames. These large sliding doors also feature on the front of the guest house, so that in the winter months the house can be shut up completely and protected from the elements.

With multiple buildings, extensive outdoor spaces and light in abundance, this Montauk residence has a sense of relaxed vibrancy that is present throughout.

OPPOSITE ABOVE: Sunlight streams through the kitchen window of the guest house, which doubles as a pool house in the summer. There is ample space for entertaining as well as self-contained accommodation for friends.

LEFT: The swimming pool, with the guest house beyond, is tucked discreetly into the sloping landscape and is within easy reach of the main house.

ABOVE: The large open-plan kitchen and living space mimics the layout of the main house but on a smaller scale. This was all part of the architect's plan that each of the buildings should relate and have similar elements while maintaining their own identities and functions.

RIGHT: Coral on display in a hurricane lantern is a reminder of the house's location, nestled between lake and ocean.

OPPOSITE: Exposed beams and rafters together with original wooden-clad walls and floors create a moody backdrop to the vast open-plan living space.

RIGHT: A private deck is used as a pit stop on the way to the beach. Its comfortable seating and stunning view make it the ideal place to relax and enjoy the idyllic surroundings.

FAR RIGHT: Rising above the dunes, the shingled roof has been painted white on the south-facing ocean side so as to keep the house cooler during the warm summer months.

SEA DRIFTS AND SAND DUNES

The exterior of Seadrift, Rick Livingston and Jim Brawders' summer escape among the sand dunes of Quogue, Long Island, reveals little of its rich history. The barn-like structure looks as if it was built exactly where it stands today, its brown-shingled façade having absorbed long hours of sunshine and endured many winter rainstorms. However, its origins are hundreds of miles away in Delaware, where it served as an army recreation hall. The building was dismantled after the First World War and moved to its current location, where it was reassembled to provide an artist's studio and beach house for a family whose summer residence was a few miles inland.

Further surprises await, with the most charming point of access being the magical private entrance from an exquisite white sandy beach. Once you have ventured inside, the interior space presents an enticing display of

ABOVE: Doors from the living area open onto a rear porch on the ocean side of the house. The decked path through the grass-covered dunes leads directly to the beach.

colour and texture, dominated by a vast open-plan space. The moody interiors challenge conventional notions regarding the decoration of a home at the water's edge. Indeed, this house is a refreshing demonstration of boldness and creativity.

Rick and Jim spent many years renting Seadrift during the summer months before finally making their dream come true and buying it. They are the longest-standing occupants that the house has ever had, and the intimacy this shared history produces has enabled a gentle, gradual and idiosyncratic approach to its interior design.

After its dramatic relocation from Delaware, the house's basic structure had been left more or less intact. Original tongue-and-groove-clad walls and bare wooden floors are the backdrop for an interior that speaks of the owners' personal styles and interests. Evident to any visitor is Rick's love of texture and layering, which meshes with his partner Jim's passion for boats and 1920s and 1930s cruise-liner travel.

Rick is a respected interior designer and antiques dealer. His creative influences can be traced back to his formative years in the fashion industry – a certain flamboyance is apparent here, and he feels entirely at

OPPOSITE FAR LEFT: A new window is the only addition Rick and Jim made to this early twentieth-century building, which is otherwise still in its original state. A daybed and comfortable reading chairs are arranged in front of it to catch the light and the sunset.

OPPOSITE ABOVE RIGHT: Fabrics and textures have been combined to create a layered effect and each of the seating areas in the open-plan interior has a different but complementary scheme. Found at antiques fairs and markets, artwork relating to the ocean has been lovingly collected by the owners.

RIGHT: The large skylight provides an additional source of natural light. A variety of seating areas have been arranged around the room, creating interest and diversity within the open space.

home 'dressing up' a space, while skilfully ensuring that it remains a place for rest and relaxation.

The house's humble origins are still evident in certain respects. There is no air conditioning, no insulation and only minimal electric lighting. A single additional window was added to increase the flow of light and showcase the glorious sunsets, and the interior is primarily an open space with bedrooms tucked away at one end and a small enclosed kitchen at the other. The front of the house on the beach side has a the prettiest of porches nestled in a cleft in the hilly dunes, and the grass and sand stretching beyond to the beach is Rick and Jim's own private 'garden'. They also added a deck with comfortable seating at the top of the dunes and cheerfully confess that they rarely make it all the way to the beach.

OPPOSITE AND ABOVE LEFT: The dining space at one end of the room boasts a set of 1920s vintage chairs. An old tin locker has found a new purpose as a linen cupboard, and a fanciful raffia chandelier, customized by the owner, hangs proudly above the table.

ABOVE: A huge collection of shells and corals is on display throughout the house; their intriguing tones and textures provided inspiration for the interior colour scheme.

There are stories associated with most of Rick's acquisitions. Items have been collected on his travels and at antiques fairs. Many were chance finds while he was sourcing on behalf of clients. His collection of vintage apple-picking ladders is the perfect example of this. A dealer was selling them individually, and Rick promptly purchased the lot. This cluster of ladders works decoratively as a large-scale art installation but they also have a practical purpose, as they are used to access the roof space.

Other original collections give this house soul. Abundant shell displays have been so intricately arranged and lit that they pass as still lifes. Die-cut cross sections of steam passenger ships found in Louis Vuitton trunks are beautifully framed to line a bedroom wall. There are vintage models of ships dotted around the place, since Jim is an avid collector, but there is nothing

contrived about these. Beautifully executed, rather than a clichéd decorating idea for a house with coastal connotations, they look like they belong here. Birdcages hang en masse above the centrally located table-tennis table, all different shapes and sizes but all painted vibrant orange, while postcards that Rick received from his parents when he was a boy have been made into a collage on the closet doors.

Another item that adds a playful element to the interior space and illustrates Rick's creativity is the whimsical chandelier that hangs above the dining space. The bare raffia pendant was purchased in New York and the tassels came from St Barts and Trinidad. Once the two were combined, Rick had this splendid creation wired up to the electricity supply and finished it with candles that are lit when the couple have guests.

OPPOSITE ABOVE AND BELOW: The master bedroom is decorated in muted tones. A vintage floral rug offers contrast to more masculine stripes. Postcards collected by the owner during his childhood are displayed on the wooden closet doors.

ABOVE: The turquoise ceiling in the spare bedroom is reminiscent of the colour of the nearby ocean. Old louvred doors were reinstalled here as wall panels.

This house is all about layers. Rick is fanatical about texture and colour, and inspiration is drawn from shells, coral and the beach grass that surrounds the house. Browns and subtle oranges – all muted in tone, as if weathered by the elements – have been carefully selected. Splashes of vibrant blue and pale grey echoing the sea and the sky also make an appearance. Textures such as raffia, linens and vintage crewel sit as beautifully on rusting vintage furniture as they do on newly upholstered pieces.

The interior space, while primarily open plan, is also a collection of different areas for reading, for conversation, for dining and for relaxing. So while the open space may appear to lack privacy, the way the furniture has been arranged means that you can get away from it all while remaining in easy calling distance.

Seadrift has moved greatly in terms of time, distance and atmosphere since its genesis in distant Delaware, but it retains connotations of the era in which it was constructed. It is fortunate to have owners such as Rick and Jim, who have maintained the building's essential elements and infused them with great soul and spirit by adding inspiring personal touches.

OPPOSITE ABOVE: The front porch that faces the ocean is surrounded by sand dunes and beach vegetation. A mixture of modern teak loungers and old French metal rocking chairs illustrates the clever combination of styles that characterizes this house.

OPPOSITE BELOW: The three metal globes in the garden are made from wagon wheel treads.

ABOVE RIGHT: A patriotic display in front of the main entrance porch.

RIGHT: Beach fencing zigzags through the sand in front of the property.

FAR RIGHT: The rustic outdoor shower.

OPPOSITE ABOVE LEFT: An infinity swimming pool was sited discreetly at the far end of the house, close to the covered verandah to enable use in all weather conditions.

OPPOSITE ABOVE RIGHT: Rattan furniture provides additional seating on the lawn area between the two terraces.

OPPOSITE BELOW: Oak-leaved hydrangeas in oversized pots join a grapevine that's starting to scramble over the huge pergola.

ABOVE RIGHT: A seventeeth-century Basque door made of oak, found in the Navarra region of Spain, is the main entrance to the house.

RIGHT: The swimming pool can be reached directly from the guest bedroom, through a gated window.

When Madrid-based interior designer Isabel López-Quesada was shown La Faisanderie, a run-down farmhouse set in oak woods and rolling hills just outside Biarritz in south-west France, she knew at once that it was going to be her home. The building stood at the heart of a working pheasant farm and was barely habitable, but Isabel recognized its potential and bought it straight away.

LA CÔTE DES BASQUES

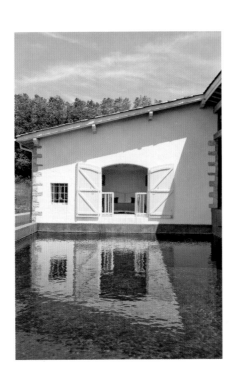

Given the dilapidated state of the old farmhouse, many would have carried out a comprehensive renovation before moving in. But instead Isabel gave a small section of the house a coat of paint, installed a temporary kitchen and bathroom and spent the first summer 'camping' in the incomplete surrounds with her young family. It was one of the best summers they ever had.

This modest living arrangement enabled Isabel to develop an intimate awareness of the site and to realize how she might transform the humble farmhouse into something very special. The consequence of this gently paced introduction of house to owner is a combination of space, light and division that gives enduring pleasure to family and visitors alike.

When the renovation began, Isabel started by repositioning the house on the land. The west, sea-facing side of the building was originally a long closed length of wall, providing no access to

the panoramic views of the valley below and towards the nearby Atlantic coast. A series of windows was inserted into this wall and Isabel added a long terrace that now overlooks wonderful landscaping by the renowned Spanish garden designer Fernando Caruncho.

Next, a second building was added, connected to the original farmhouse by a newly constructed entrance area and a huge drawing room. These open, airy spaces now link the guest pavilion, swimming pool and second terrace to the main house. This new section was primarily designed for entertaining guests and socializing, but the new additions also enabled the house to be more centred on its plot.

The house is painted white with shuttered windows – typical of the Basque architecture in this area of France. To comply with stringent planning guidelines, most of the buildings dotted amongst these hills have dark red

OPPOSITE ABOVE: The entrance area is paved in old terracotta roof tiles that the owner found in Provençe. It adjoins a large salon area, with a contrasting floor of polished concrete. A 'floating' staircase made of untreated oak was designed so as not to interrupt the openness of this space.

OPPOSITE BELOW: A large piece of coral – chosen for its form, colour and texture – has a sculptural presence in a gallery-like environment.

RIGHT: Parts of the original walls were left exposed in the renovation, conveying a sense of the house's long history.

BELOW RIGHT: An antique desk is used as stand-alone bookcase.

BELOW: The view from below the open staircase includes the entrance hall and the doorway to the bright and airy drawing room.

or green shutters, but Isabel was determined that hers should be pale grey. As a result, the Farrow & Ball shade that she chose has now been added to the list of certified colours that can be used in the area, and the fresh white and grey combination is the epitome of summery perfection.

Two huge terraces are attached to the house. One, close to the infinity swimming pool that is concealed behind the guest pavilion, is covered so it can be used whatever the weather. This terrace includes a myriad of beautiful seating areas and planting, resembling an enormous garden room without walls, and is situated close to the galley kitchen in the guest area, which doubles as a pool house in the summer months. It is full of inviting armchairs, squashy sofas and chaise longues, and you can imagine whiling away long summer afternoons here. Striped ticking fabrics are mixed with faded florals, while cane and rattan chairs sit companionably alongside beautifully weathered teak. The mix of materials, textures and styles create layers of interest and beauty. Verdant planting in simple terracotta pots and galvanized metal containers make this the perfect outdoor room.

The other terrace is more open to the elements and adjoins the kitchen, which is situated in the original part of the house. This is the hub of the home, where the family congregate and spend most of their time. There is a mix of seating areas for eating, conversing or relaxing. Grapevines planted in oversized terracotta pots and vintage wine barrels are being trained over

OPPOSITE: A simple wooden table and bench seating give the kitchen a clean, modern feel, with a vintage industrial pendant as a centrepiece. Doors on either side allow natural light to flood in throughout the day.

ABOVE: Oak wood is used throughout the house; simple steps that mirror the main staircase lead from the kitchen into the salon.

ABOVE RIGHT: In the utility room next to the kitchen, an old table has been transformed into a sink unit with open shelving. On either side, shelves are concealed behind floor-to-ceiling curtains.

the pergola, which is made of stone pillars and oak beams. Moroccan-style copper lanterns have been wired overhead to provide soft mood lighting in the evenings. During the summer months, the family eat breakfast, lunch and dinner on this pleasantly open, breezy terrace.

The scale, light and volume of the interior are impressive. The vast drawing room – the room that sits between the two outdoor living areas – boasts floor-to-ceiling glass doors and windows that open out onto the garden. It is full of natural light and has beautiful views. Vases filled with oak leaves and vines bring the outside in and add lush greenery to the space. External blinds made of willow provide a rustic solution to the dazzling midday sun and complement the pretty landscaping.

In the main entrance salon, a new floating oak staircase provides a simple, architectural focal point. Modern in design, it is open so as not to obstruct the sense of flow. It leads to the master bedroom and bathroom on the first floor and the children's rooms tucked into the eaves at the top of the house.

Simple materials have been used throughout the interior; a skilful combination of old and new items. Smooth concrete floors have been laid in much of the house, a wax coating ensuring comfort beneath bare feet. Salvaged terracotta ceiling tiles from Provençe were used to create the floor in the entrance hall, while the wood planks in the drawing room are reclaimed drying shelves from a porcelain factory in England and have been joined with cement to fill the holes, creating a unique effect. Slate planks that were once oyster plantation beds from the Ile de Ré adorn the wide expanse of the covered terrace floor. They are laid in a classic finger-pattern parquetry design, and the remnants of marine life add a wonderful texture to the finish. Mixing the floor materials throughout adds interest and variety to the interior – an experiment that is easily carried off in a house of this scale.

ABOVE LEFT: Children's bedrooms have been slotted into previously disused attic areas, while the original roof structure of the building is a feature of the master bedroom (above).

ABOVE AND OPPOSITE: Parts of the original stone walls were left exposed to keep a sense of the building's past. New windows were added to optimize glorious views of the coast.

The large drawing room is airy and bright with white-painted walls, ceilings and stairs leading up to the main entrance hall. Windows open onto the garden. The capacious custom-made sofa was designed to offset the volume of the room and sits comfortably alongside a mix of vintage and second-hand seating, upholstered in a variety of different fabrics.

LEFT AND BELOW LEFT: Instead of the usual cut flowers, the owner likes to use armfuls of lush foliage from the garden to make a dramatic statement in the drawing room and entrance hall.

On the same day that Isabel bought the house, she started shopping at antiques markets and fairs. Furniture, textiles, old doors, plant pots, rugs, tiles – anything that caught her eye and she liked has found its way into her design. The centuries-old door that now provides an entrance to the house, for example, was discovered in Navarra, in Spain. When Isabel found and fell in love with some antique tiles, it turned out that there were not enough of them to complete a floor in any of the rooms, so she inlaid what she had into the concrete floor and now they make an unusual and beautiful focal point in the guest bathroom. All these diverse materials and objects have their own history, and they bring the interior alive.

The house has been stylishly decorated with an eclectic, cleverly combined mixture of fabrics, textures and furniture. Isabel loves natural linen fabrics and uses old and new alike. These allow the house to feel summery and relaxed. Collections of shells and marine life provide textural displays, among them a pair of whale ribs and a giant piece of coral, which look as if they could be pieces of sculpture in a modern gallery.

Isabel says that the best thing about La Faisanderie is the amount of light that floods into the interior, as well as the very large and luxurious proportions of the rooms. For her, these are the elements that give the house its sense of elegant sophistication, not merely the furniture or objects or the decoration within. The real luxury for Isabel was to be able to build this whole house – her beloved haven – to her very own taste and style, exactly how she wanted it to be.

ABOVE: Exterior blinds of slatted willow were made to fit the large drawing-room windows and offer a smart solution for controlling both sun and shade.

RIGHT: A sleekly unobtrusive infinity pool is concealed behind the guest pavilion, close to the covered terrace and accessible from the garden. The covered terrace adjoins a galley kitchen on the other side; this doubles as a pool house on sunny summer days.

OPPOSITE: The frontage of Wonoma Lodge, as seen from the Boathouse, which is located just a few yards away on the other side of the gravel road. The widow's walk is a striking feature common to many houses in the area.

RIGHT AND FAR RIGHT: The deck at the rear of the house sits at the base of the sand dunes, with a sandy beach on the other side.

BELOW RIGHT: On the other side of the house, another outdoor area allows direct access to the beach over the dunes; there is a further seating area that catches the morning sun.

A STEP BACK IN TIME

Arriving in Nantucket, the picturesque island off the coast of Cape Cod in Massachusetts, feels like stepping back in time. The island boasts the largest concentration of pre-Civil War houses in the United States, most of which have been painstakingly restored. Cobblestones line many of the streets, and homes that have been handed down through the generations maintain their historical integrity. Traditional grey-shingled exteriors, gabled roofs and crisp white trims meet the eye at every turn, a result of stringent planning guidelines. All these factors contribute to making it a strangely perfect place.

Wonoma Lodge and the Boathouse stand on a narrow stretch of land on the north-east point of Nantucket island. Wonoma faces the harbour and backs onto the ocean behind it. The Boathouse is barely a stone's throw away, across a gravel road.

When the current owners bought Wonoma Lodge and began renovating the cottage, they wanted to respect the true essence of Nantucket, its history

ABOVE AND ABOVE RIGHT: Classic Nantucket cottage style is very much in evidence throughout the house, with tongue-and-groove walls and ceilings and wooden floorboards, all painted in a glossy finish to reflect the natural light. Painted floors are a typical feature of old Nantucket houses.

OPPOSITE: The cottage furniture is a mixture of locally sourced items that reflect the maritime history of the island and hand-finished, painted wooden pieces that were custom made for the house.

as a former whaling town and the ethos of cottage living. Built in the 1930s, it was originally the honeymoon cottage of Wauwinet House, a charming historic inn in the town of Wauwinet. The house's footprint has remained as it was, but the rooms have been slightly reconfigured in order to accommodate an extra bedroom and bathroom. Outdoor space was redesigned and dormer windows were added to the upstairs rooms to enhance the light and the view.

The owners also added a widow's walk to the cottage roof – a railed platform that is a traditional design feature of New England coastal houses built in

ABOVE: Dormer windows in the bedroom provide additional light and idyllic views. Locally made woven fabrics and antique quilts dress a pair of wrought-iron beds.

LEFT: A custom-designed linen cabinet and old ship's ladder, used to access the widow's walk, tuck neatly into an upstairs nook.

the eighteenth and early nineteenth centuries. These observation decks earned their names from the wives of mariners, who would patiently watch and wait for the return of their husbands' fishing boats. Today, the widow's walk provides panoramic views across the grassy dunes to both harbour and ocean beyond.

Together with local interior decorator Janet Kielley, the owners decided on a blend of muted tones and colours inspired by the cottage's maritime environment. Blues and greens echo the subtle shades of sea and beach grass. Wood-panelled walls and doors were painted in varying shades of the same colour –

a calming effect of tone on tone. Painted floors – historically significant and in keeping with the style of old Nantucket houses – were base-coated then topped with three or four layers of high-gloss deck paint, a beautiful finish that only improves with age.

Much of the furniture was sourced locally, including a ship's ladder that accesses the widow's walk through a trapdoor from the second floor. Custom-made throws from local weavers are piled alongside antique quilts, and objects recalling the island's past are mixed with driftwood and shells collected from surrounding beaches.

The Boathouse also originally belonged to Wauwinet House and once performed the function that its name suggests. When it came up for sale, the owners of Wonoma Lodge decided to buy it to provide accommodation for guests and a place their adult daughters could call their own. They were eager to respect the history of the structure and many boathouse details were referenced when it came to restoring the interior.

In contrast to Wonoma, the Boathouse already had a widow's walk, which was removed to fit in a second floor. The original height remained, and the kitchen and living areas were installed in this section of the house, opening onto a balcony along one side with spectacular harbour views. Directly below is a covered porch – a relaxing spot on which to spend time.

ABOVE RIGHT: The shingled façade of the Boathouse is very similar to that of Wonoma Lodge. The path to its front entrance is cut through the luxuriant beach grass that dominates the surrounding landscape.

RIGHT: The entrance to the Boathouse reveals its palette of light colours and pale wood. Wooden shutters control the light and provide privacy and shade when necessary.

When considering the interiors, the owners wanted the cottage to feel as if it had always been there and were mindful of this when choosing beams, floorboards, hardware and cabinetry. Distressed, chalky wall finishes were used, and muted tones reminiscent of the colours of the ocean give a warm and authentic feel to the interior spaces. Reclaimed oak floorboards in varying widths were installed and buffed with an oil-based soap finish, providing a smooth feeling underfoot.

Many objects with nautical associations were added to the rooms to enhance the boathouse feel. These include a set of vintage oars, a large wooden propeller tipped with oxidized zinc, and caged industrial light fittings – a nod to the 'onion lamps' traditionally used in Nantucket interiors. Weathered items found during walks along the beach such as

OPPOSITE: The living area opens onto a balcony with views over the harbour. Reclaimed oak floorboards were buffed with an oil-based soap finish giving them a traditional feel. A cushioned banquette runs along one side of the dining table, while locally made dining chairs complete the arrangement.

ABOVE AND ABOVE LEFT: The kitchen has a cottagey feel, with its simple design, open shelving and whitewashed wood-clad walls.

ABOVE AND ABOVE RIGHT: Neutrals and subtle blues dominate the colour palette in the living area. Chunky linens, worn wood and nubbly jute rugs bring texture and interest to the interior. While white-painted shutters have been used on most of the windows, a few were left uncovered to allow light to flood in. Roman blinds made of woven grass fabric combined with shutters were fitted in the bedrooms to add warmth and texture.

OPPOSITE: A traditional bobbin bed was found in one of the antique shops on the island. It is layered with a variety of textural linens, also sourced locally.

driftwood, striped stones and shells are displayed as decorative collections. Striped fabrics in blues and greys or browns and greys were chosen over the classic blue and white, giving a modern twist.

These two residences epitomize comfortable present-day living using designs, furnishings and colours that reflect the history of the buildings themselves and the history of Nantucket. The clever use of local artefacts and products is combined with an emphasis on appropriate restoration and quality workmanship, and an understanding that a modern home can be created without leaving the past behind.

OPPOSITE ABOVE LEFT AND RIGHT: The narrow stretch of land that is Fire Island has ocean waves on one side and calm bay waters on the other, both within easy walking distance via its wooden boardwalks and sandy paths.

OPPOSITE BELOW: The front entrance to the house is a covered porch. Afternoon sun streams through the windows, and ceiling fans keep things cool.

RIGHT AND FAR RIGHT The calm, tranquil bay where the ferry from the mainland docks. Wagons are left at the wharf, enabling easy transportation of luggage and supplies in this car-free hamlet.

TO THE LIGHTHOUSE

Making your way to Fire Island feels like a chronological journey as well as a geographical one. There is much pleasure to be gained from the ferry itself, which offers a view of the island's striped black and white lighthouse. And arriving at Saltaire, the tranquil village where the ferry docks, feels like a step back in time, mainly due to the fact there are no paved roads or motor vehicles here.

One of the most charming aspects of this island hamlet is the lack of modern amenities. Apart from two churches, a yacht club, a library and a small market, Saltaire is primarily residential, with an exquisite stretch of white sandy beach on the opposite side of the island to the jetty. There are no cars on the island, but everything is within easy walking or cycling distance. The streets are a series of boardwalk promenades, enabling these modes of transport. With a year-round population of fewer than fifty, most of the inhabitants are summer dwellers with holiday homes here and residents take pride in the island's family atmosphere.

ABOVE: A striking lighthouse, with distinctive black and white stripes, is located at the far end of the island and is accessed on foot via sandy paths.

RIGHT AND FAR RIGHT: Visitors ring an old handbell to signal their arrival, and an assortment of playful signs hangs by the front door.

BELOW: The internal porch window looks back into the master bedroom.

The houses that are nestled amongst the beach grass and foliage in between the raised boardwalks are, in the main, wonderful examples of old cedar-shingled beach houses. Many of these are 'Coffey Houses', deriving their name from Irish builder Mike Coffey, who settled on the island in the 1920s. He built many of the early homes, which are solid in appearance and characterized by a triple vertical windowpane pattern in the upper part of the window (referred to locally as 'eyebrow' windows). Many of these houses were demolished in the great hurricane of 1938, but some survived and remain in use today. New architectural styles have also emerged on the island, most of them honouring the legacy of Mike Coffey.

OPPOSITE: The light, cosy porch is surrounded by external windows and is flooded with sunshine on fine days. The deep, custom-made daybeds with their plump, linen-upholstered cushions provide a comfortable place for relaxation, as well as extra sleeping space for guests.

Alex and Andrew Bates have been holiday residents of Saltaire for many years, initially renting other houses then buying this idyllic holiday home. Its architecture is typical of the area, and the house is just a short walk from where the ferry docks. The front entrance, via a private boardwalk, is a charming enclosed porch. The cedar shingles on the façade are continued into the interior of this room. They are stained chocolate brown and contrast vividly with the crisp, white-painted floor, ceiling and window frames. Slowly rotating ceiling fans give a faint suggestion of colonial times.

This entrance porch doubles as a sitting room, complete with inviting built-in window seats that can be used as beds when the house is full of guests. Sun streams in the windows and one can imagine falling asleep there on a lazy afternoon with a good book in hand. When it starts to get cooler, the throws come out and the porch becomes a cosy and relaxing space that can be used in all weather conditions.

Alex and Andrew changed little of the house, which was designed in the early part of the twentieth century. They retained the floor plan and the original kitchen. Apart from replacing old tiles with wainscoting, they kept everything just as it was when they bought it, including the blue linoleum kitchen floor – a bolt of colour within the white interior.

The main priority for this house was to keep things simple and low maintenance – their idea of what a holiday home should be about. Washable white cotton slipcovers adorn the furniture, most of which is second hand. The shiny finish to walls and floors comes from high-gloss paint, while sisal and jute rugs complete the seaside feel in the living spaces.

There are three small bedrooms – a bunk room adjacent to the entrance and two others inside. The master bedroom has windows that open directly onto the porch. All are simply decorated with white linens and the odd burst of ocean colour.

When it comes to decorating, Alex thinks more in terms of collecting. From the collection of retro fans in the porch to the stack of perfectly placed vintage tennis rackets just inside the front door, everything feels like it belongs here. Antique turtle shells adorn a wall – relics from an earlier time – while pebbles, shells and antlers shed by the local island deer create interesting vignettes throughout. All these elements reflect Alex's personal style and creativity.

LEFT: The kitchen is reached from the living room via a narrow arched opening that frames the striking blue floor and the farmhouse-style table and chairs.

OPPOSITE ABOVE: A plate rack is stacked with pretty oyster platters, providing a visual display behind the table.

OPPOSITE BELOW LEFT: A collection of white American pottery from the 1930 and 1940s finds a place on the top of the painted cabinet. The variety of textures, shapes and sizes ensures the success of the white-on-white approach.

OPPOSITE BELOW RIGHT: In the kitchen, Alex retained the original glossy blue linoleum flooring. It provides a vibrant contrast to the otherwise all-white interior.

An avid collector, Alex often returns from holidays laden down with bags full of exciting finds. Rugs, baskets and hats are treasured souvenirs of straw markets in the Bahamas, and furniture and objects often make their way back from the flea markets of Paris and antiques fairs in Massachusetts. Wampum beads – traditional sacred shells of the indigenous people of North America – have also been collected locally. Alex loves them for their purple and mauve colouring, and the beautiful patterns they possess.

Alex and Andrew's house is a sanctuary within the sanctuary that is Fire Island's Saltaire. Personal, intimate, stylish and livable, it reflects the essential characteristics of one of this area's most outstanding locations.

OPPOSITE: Corrugated tin, recycled from the original building, lines the walls and ceiling of the drawing room. Rough concrete floors recall the structure's previous use, and furnishings are a collection of pre-loved treasures, cleverly combined to create a comfortable environment.

ABOVE LEFT: Cedar shingles and weathered eucalyptus planking on the exterior walls create an interplay of textures and shapes.

ABOVE RIGHT: Three salvaged French windows have been turned into doors and offer an alternative entrance to the drawing room.

RIGHT: A set of wooden barn doors opens up at one end of the porch, retaining a sense of the pheasant coop that the building once was.

HOME TO ROOST

In contrast to the luxurious interiors she designs for clients, Isabel López-Quesada wanted to get back to basics and make things simple for this project, a guest house in the grounds of her own holiday home just outside Biarritz in southern France (see pages 94–107). It is fondly known as 'the Hen House', since it was previously part of a large pheasant farm. Everything used to build and furnish this house was found, inherited or donated; its special quality comes from the view, the light and the simplicity.

When Isabel bought the property, there were 14 run-down hen coops and 30,000 pheasants dotting the surrounding meadows. Only someone with her extraordinary vision could envisage transforming one of the dingy coops into a beautiful, eclectic and cosy dwelling for guests.

PREVIOUS PAGE: The deep covered porch is a shady retreat that runs along the entire side of the house. Furnished with comfortable wicker sofas, this is an idyllic place to sit and relax. The original steps into the pheasant coop have been retained and lead to the bedrooms.

ABOVE: Old wicker baskets sit alongside giant lanterns and an antique birdcage on a long, zinc-topped console table.

LEFT: Pretty planting and stacks of old terracotta pots add to the air of rustic charm.

Yet this is exactly what she has achieved. Isabel's extended family fight to spend time there, arriving with wetsuits and surfboards in the summer and always reluctant to leave.

All of the pheasant coops were demolished except for the largest and best situated. Built of concrete and tin, the structure was less than salubrious. However, Isabel's vision was to convert it into a traditional barn-style building. Apart from the drawing room, which was added to the far end of the building, everything else was original, yet transformed.

The exterior was clad in eucalyptus wood panels, which weather to a soft grey colour, while cedar shingles on the roof were given a similarly beautiful effect thanks to the elements. Doors and windows salvaged from the nearby main house were added, and when more doors were needed, old shutters were converted for the purpose.

The original wooden structure was retained and insulated with recycled woollens. A concrete floor was laid and the interior walls were lined with pine timber. Corrugated tin was used to line the walls in the sitting room, artfully patchworked together with extraordinary effect. Grey and rusted in parts, the tin is spectacular and strange at the same time.

With a vastly expanding collection of discarded materials from clients' sites, furniture that friends and family no longer wanted and anything anybody was giving away, Isabel had plenty of cast-offs to add to the cabin. Nothing was wasted or spared – this project was done on a tight budget, and Isabel found a home for everything. When panels for the exterior were too wide, they were cut down and the remaining pieces were used to cover the floor of the porch.

RIGHT, ABOVE AND BELOW: The bedrooms open onto the long covered porches that run along each side of the house, and can be accessed both internally and externally. Walls and ceilings are lined with pine and painted white, except for the original structural beams, which were left in their natural state, to add interest and contrast. White bed linen conveys a crisp, summery feel, and vintage quilts and blankets from around the world give each bedroom an individual style.

ABOVE: The master bedroom and bathroom is one large open space, designed to make a feature of a freestanding shower that was purchased before the project began. Unfinished concrete flooring enhances the sculptural feeling of this unique piece. It also enabled the shower to be fitted directly to the floor, without a base or plinth.

ABOVE RIGHT: A chair upholstered in French vintage fabric, specially designed washstands and a deep bathtub built beneath the window and clad in wooden planking, make this guest bathroom a desirable place to linger.

Affordable pine was used for the interior, and everything that needed covering up was given a coat of white paint. Her carpenter also constructed a simple wooden kitchen cabinet to keep costs down.

The result is charming. Apart from plans that were drawn up for the spatial arrangements, everything else evolved spontaneously during Isabel's visits to the site. The temporary stairs built for work during construction were kept and now form a central element of the design, linking the drawing room to the rest of the house. Isabel's style is evident throughout – the mix of vintage and ethnic fabrics, well-considered bathrooms with bathtubs and washstands clad in wood, a psychedelic rug from Argentina transformed into a coffee table that, against all expectations, sits comfortably with French iron doors and nineteenth-century chairs.

The central corridor is painted white – floors, walls and ceilings – to dramatic effect. Light streams in from above, flooding through the original ventilation that was in place for the pheasants, while simple, utilitarian, wall-mounted lights illuminate a row of mounted antlers.

ABOVE: Pine boards line the interior walls and are painted white throughout. The corridor gets its light from the glassed-in openings beneath the eaves, which originally provided ventilation for the pheasants. A row of white antlers and deer heads give a gallery feel to the space.

ABOVE RIGHT AND RIGHT: The kitchen cabinetry is utilitarian in design and constructed from inexpensive pine. The furniture throughout is a mix of donated and inherited pieces. Every item in this house has a story attached to it, right down to the china, most of which is on display on open shelves.

ABOVE: The drawing room is the only new addition to the original structure, but all of the materials used in its construction are either recycled or have been reused. A rough patchwork of corrugated tin lines the walls, and the stairs that link this room with the rest of the house were hastily knocked up by the builders during construction but have become a permanent fixture.

The bedrooms all lead off this central corridor and can be accessed either internally or from the covered porches that run along both sides of the rectangular structure. The steps leading up to the roosts that the farmer once used to gain access to the birds have been retained and now serve as external access points to the bedrooms.

The master bedroom at the end of the corridor is a large open space incorporating a bathroom. A black, cylindrical shower made of fibre cement sits in one corner of the room. Isabel found it at a Paris design fair and it is her homage to the minimalist sculptor Richard Serra. It was purchased before work started on the house and she knew it would be the highlight of any room, making sure that its home was in an open and exposed area.

The larger of the two porches faces south and is bathed in beautiful sunlight for much of the day. It is very deep, and a series of comfortable seating areas and dining spaces make it into an additional room. Terracotta

pots, old wooden crates and galvanized metal planters are overflowing with luscious greenery, while vines are starting to clamber into the eaves. Deep sofas and chairs are upholstered in soft linens and adorned with plump cushions. Rattan furniture mixed with vintage metals combine to make this outdoor setting hard to leave.

The outside area and the surrounding gardens have also been transformed, thanks to the magic touch of celebrated Spanish landscape designer Fernando Caruncho. Small oaks were planted to supplement the older ones, along with abundant jasmine, hydrangeas and trailing roses. The cabin has a magical feel, both inside and out – testament to Isabel's vision, imagination and great resourcefulness. And despite her stipulation to the previous owners that they must remove all the pheasants and their cages from the property when they left, one or two remain and roam around the area contentedly, as if they entirely approve of the changes she has wrought.

ABOVE LEFT: The corrugated tin, rusted in parts, makes a textural backdrop for furniture and simple displays. Lighting is subtle, to blend in with the rustic nature of the room.

ABOVE: A set of three windows originally from an old French warehouse and purchased in a Paris flea market were converted into doors that flood the room with soft, natural light. Each has a smaller window within the panel that can be opened separately.

OPPOSITE ABOVE LEFT: A decked terrace next to the main living area serves as an extra room. The dining table and bench seating is made from untreated wood and white-painted metal. Cushions for comfort and rugs for cooler days are always on hand.

OPPOSITE ABOVE RIGHT: A garden of roses and lavender creates a country-cottage effect. The black and white exterior colour scheme is typical of cabins in this area.

OPPOSITE BELOW: A central decked entrance area divides the cabin in two; bedrooms are on one side and living areas on the other.

RIGHT: The kitchen windows overlook the pretty garden.

ABOVE RIGHT: Blue-and-white striped bathing huts line the nearby shore.

A coat of black paint transformed the exterior of this Danish cabin, close to the Baltic Sea on the north Sjælland coast. It was once brown, both inside and out, but when Tine Kjeldsen and her husband Jacob Fossum moved in, they repainted the exterior so it was more in keeping with the typical summerhouses of the area. Inside, they used generous amounts of white paint to cover walls, ceilings and woodwork, creating a light, bright and breezy interior.

A COASTAL CABIN

As well as painting the interior, the only additional work undertaken was to build a large terrace next to the existing living space. Undercover yet open to the elements, this is an all-important aspect of Danish summerhouse tradition, appealing to the Scandinavian love of being outdoors regardless of the weather conditions. The terrace, effectively an extra room, has a large dining table as its focal point and is where the couple and their children always eat, even when it rains. During the long summer days experienced at this latitude, this area is in constant use.

The rest is an expression of Tine's own personal style and her ability to decorate in a simple, uncluttered way. After all, she is at the creative helm of her eponymous homewares

ABOVE AND ABOVE RIGHT: A piece of fallen wood from the nearby forest rests casually against a wall to create a simple decorative element in the living room. White cotton canvas slipcovers provide a casual, beachy feel, made more chic by a scattering of textured cushions and a warm throw.

business, Tine K Home. Her collections of cushions and quilts have a minimalist yet comfortable feel. She prefers clean lines and colours in varying shades of grey, blue, white and black, as illustrated by her constantly expanding range that now includes interior products, furniture and textiles, as well as clothing.

Tine's intention for her summerhouse was to create a place where she and her young family could completely relax and switch off from their hectic city lives; a place that was easy to be in and easy to look after. The outcome is a stylish, casual and livable home that the whole family escapes to every summer. Rooms are simply decorated and low maintenance. Candles and lanterns are dotted around, their flickering, atmospheric light preferred

to electrical options. A large, squashy sofa, on which the whole family can snuggle up together and watch movies if it rains, has a simple, washable white cotton slipcover and is furnished with layer upon layer of plump cushions from her collections.

Tine's colour preferences are evident throughout. Painted floorboards in a warm grey shade add contrast to the white walls and ceilings. The wooden dining table is painted high-gloss white, and the black Eames chairs that surround it give a sharp, graphic look. This is softened by small arrangements that Tine creates on tables, window sills and any available horizontal surface, as well as vases of flowers gathered from the abundant garden that surrounds the house.

ABOVE: An old wooden table was spray painted to a glossy white finish. Books are piled high at the end of the bench seat – a fun idea as an alternative to built-in shelving or bookcases. Grey-painted floorboards and white walls and ceilings are grounded by the splashes of black and charcoal introduced by the vintage furniture and cabinetry.

LEFT: The simple grey and white colour scheme unifies the interior. Straw baskets inside the front door are an ideal storage solution for shoes, hats and beach towels.

BELOW LEFT: The kitchen overlooks the pretty garden. A large, open-shelved cabinet keeps everyday items within arm's reach. Striped ticking curtains replace cupboard doors.

The furniture is a combination of Tine's own products, design classics and French antiques. She likes to mix old and new, painted and raw wood, and linen, velvet and cotton fabrics, working up contrasts to create an individual look that is consistent with the pieces she designs for her seasonal ranges.

This house is an secluded oasis, connected to the nearby beach by a narrow path through a small pine forest. The family often walk or cycle there, chatting, swapping stories and reminiscing about past summers. These rituals help create the emotional resonance that surrounds this gorgeous home, and are part and parcel of what living by the water should be about.

ABOVE: French doors open from the master bedroom onto the terrace. Sheer linen curtains create a soft, breezy effect.

LEFT AND OPPOSITE BELOW RIGHT: The bedrooms are simple, with wooden furniture painted white to blend with the walls. Beds are dressed in pale linens and lightweight quilts. A wooden ladder is a space-saving alternative to a clothes rail or shelving.

OPPOSITE ABOVE LEFT: Two buildings were added to the existing farmhouse, to create a new symmetry on the plot. Joined by glass breezeways, the central stone section was inspired by Midwestern barns, while the new bedroom suite mimics the original farmhouse building on the other side.

OPPOSITE ABOVE RIGHT: The glass breezeways that link the three structures allow light to spill into the interior.

OPPOSITE BELOW: The outdoor dining area at the rear of the house has a stone fireplace to allow entertaining whatever the weather.

ABOVE RIGHT: The pool house has crisp white barn doors and window frames – a contrast to the weathered cedar shingles that cover the exterior.

RIGHT: Interior walls and ceilings are clad in reclaimed mushroom wood.

Located on magnificent Shelter Island, the quiet and charming oasis that is positioned between the north and south fork of Long Island, this sophisticated farmhouse was originally intended as a beach house and weekend getaway for a family based in New York City. However, midway through the process of transforming the simple farmhouse structure into a modern but rustic hideaway, the owners decided to move there permanently.

ISLAND FARMHOUSE

The owners did not want to create a huge house nor to overwhelm the existing farmhouse building, which dated back to the early 1900s. However, at the same time they wanted a home that could comfortably accommodate family, work and social life. So, together with architects Schappacher White, they decided to create a collection of buildings inspired by Midwestern American barns. The result is a beautiful combination of rustic, easy living and modern, gallery-like entertaining spaces.

The house is made up of three distinct structures that meld harmoniously into one. Floor-to-ceiling glass breezeways seamlessly connect the original farmhouse with the new components. A new stone building is home to the central living area, which also acts as a gallery space for a collection of work by the owner and other artists. This is flanked by the original farmhouse on one side and a new

ABOVE AND LEFT: The main living area, which opens onto the outdoor dining space, has flooring of reclaimed elm wood that has been laid with traditional rose nails. Ceilings and beams are reclaimed mushroom wood, and the central fireplace is built in the same stone as the exterior of this section of the house.

OPPOSITE ABOVE AND FAR RIGHT: A freestanding pergola is constructed from powder-coated metal, with aircraft cables forming the top section. A large table was made from leftover elm wood from the living-room floors. Three industrial-style enamel pendant light fittings hang overhead.

double-height bedroom suite on the other, the exterior of which reflects the earlier building in happy symmetry.

The original two-storey farmhouse was augmented with a galley-kitchen extension and a wraparound porch. The porch is unusually deep and was designed to provide both shade from the sun and protection from the rain. Its wood-panelled ceilings are fitted with large fans to create a breeze in hot weather. It is an inviting space to escape to in the heat as well as a much-used entertaining area in bad weather.

A large outdoor dining area at the rear of the house is effectively another room. The ceiling is a wonderfully high, wisteria-covered pergola and its focal point is a large, double-sided stone fireplace, which is mirrored in the adjoining living room. It is flanked by floor-to-ceiling glass panels that connect the outdoor dining room with the indoor living room. The beautifully considered flow from inside to out is a great advantage when entertaining guests. The large outdoor dining table seats 14 and classic bistro chairs have been painted a deep caviar colour to match the steel work in the area. Large bluestone pavers define the floor area in the living room and glass breezeways, and this carries through to the pergola area to give a sense of one continuous space.

The original pool house still stands and has a boathouse feel. Large barn-like doors open at the front and back and it doubles as a guest room.

LEFT AND BELOW LEFT: Wooden sash windows run the length of the narrow galley kitchen, overlooking the back garden and outdoor dining area. Caravaggio light fittings and a zinc countertop give a contemporary feel that is tempered by the warm hues of the massive ceiling beams.

RIGHT: The pretty pool house now doubles as a guest bedroom.

The centrally positioned bed, adorned with a breezy mosquito net, is reminiscent of colonial homes in hot climates.

The property backs onto a Long Island bamboo plantation, which provides a stunning backdrop to the swimming pool. A stone retaining wall and hedge of hydrangeas was added to create privacy as well as a picturesque border. Oversized sunbeds are dotted around the pool, giving an air of beach-club glamour.

Warm natural shades have been used throughout. The owners' interest in materials and their selection of finishes has led to a wonderful combination of textures and contrasts. Floors are made of reclaimed elm, and ceilings and exposed collar ties are made of specially sourced mushroom wood, while Pennsylvanian stone lines the façade of the main building and the massive central fireplace. Cedar shingles are in keeping with the architecture of the area, and copper roofing and gutters withstand the harsh coastal weather conditions and complement the greyish tone the shingles take on over time. Zinc countertops in the kitchen and soapstone fireplaces add to list of natural materials used.

This house is a collection of traditional barn buildings, interlinked by modern glass connectors, which provide a backdrop for easy family living and entertaining. The clean lines and generous proportions coupled with dreamy landscaping and reclaimed materials create a pleasing juxtaposition of traditional and modern.

ABOVE: The tranquil swimming pool area is an oasis of calm, surrounded by lush mature planting and a wide stone surround that has ample room for sun loungers and other seating.

ABOVE RIGHT: Mosquito netting and white linen create a breezy, summery feel in the self-contained guest bedroom.

OPPOSITE: The house is nestled amongst the pines and wildflowers of this idyllic beachfront setting, with stunning views of the ocean.

RIGHT: Outdoor entertaining and shared family meals take place throughout the summer months. Piles of blankets and throws are used on chillier days.

BELOW: The large deck area of the annexe building, which is situated between the two houses, is where the two families come together for sunbathing or at mealtimes.

FAMILY HAPPINESS

Summerhouses are inevitably an important aspect of family life in Denmark, but in the case of siblings Katrine and Jannik Martensen-Larsen, their summer retreats also hold strong familial connections. Their parents built a house on land that was inherited from the pair's grandparents, and it was there that Katrine and Jannik spent their childhood summers. Katrine took over the original dwelling, and more recently her brother Jannik built a new house on the same plot to meet the needs of the next generation and their expanding families.

While the two houses are physically separate and relatively private, they are joined by an open and commonly used piece of land, allowing constant interaction between the two families during the long Scandinavian summer days. The design of the newer house is sympathetic to the original, and the two of them look as if they have always been there, side by side.

Located on Denmark's northern coastline, Nordstrand, the houses are set on a crescent-shaped strip of wide sandy beach running between the small

RIGHT: Katrine's house overlooks the ocean. The large window in the living room makes the most of the views and also ensures that the house is flooded with natural light.

BELOW: A built-in daybed with overhead shelving is a cosy, quiet place to relax with a book.

towns of Korshage and Klint. Both cabins are painted black with simple white frames for windows and doors – the traditional appearance of cottages in this area. There is also a third building on the site – an annexe used for guests, entertaining and storage.

The plot is a very much part of the landscape that surrounds it. With no fencing to delineate its boundaries, there is a sense of openness and freedom in the shared outdoor spaces and the relaxed and communal social life that they facilitate. Access to the beach is via a trail tucked away in front of the original summerhouse, and clever orientation of the new building means that the path, as well as the sea views, can be enjoyed in equal measure from both dwellings.

OPPOSITE: Tongue-and-groove panels line the walls and ceilings and are painted white throughout, with accents of black coming from the wooden table and 1950s dining chairs designed by German architect Egon Eiermann.

Katrine and Jannik's mother designed the original house. Modestly sized, it was built to a simple specification, and at first Katrine planned to enlarge it. However, she now appreciates the ease with which the house can either be opened for summer or tidied and locked up in a matter of minutes.

An open-plan kitchen and living space, a bedroom with bunks for the children, a small master bedroom and a bathroom are all fitted into a simple square footprint. On rainy days, the living room is a cosy haven, with an open fireplace and comfy seating for reading. A large square window that overlooks pines and shrubs to the sea beyond allows a stunning vista from the kitchen and living room alike.

When Katrine took over the original cottage, she changed the exterior colour from brown to black so it would harmonize with its neighbours. Renovating the inside, however, offered an opportunity for Katrine – a stylist and interior designer – to make a more individual impression. The wood-clad walls and

ceilings had yellowed with age, so the first step was to add a coat of white paint. This background showcases Katrine's preference for natural materials. The furniture and finishes she has chosen reveal an appreciation of good design and clean lines. Natural linens provide a backdrop to the bolder floral patterns selected for soft furnishings, and the crisp black accents of interior window frames, dining chairs and tables are a graphic contrast to the otherwise neutral interior.

The interior of Jannik's house echoes some of the traditional elements that feature in the original house. The wooden ceilings and walls are also painted white and contrast with dark wooden floors. The kitchen is simple and pared down. In common with Katrine's, it has a long dining table that is central to the open living and kitchen space. Both houses have the same 1950s-style dining chairs, so they can be brought together when the families host larger gatherings. Curtains have been used instead of cupboard doors – a familiar element in Danish cabin design. There is also an outdoor area for preparing food – a nod to the al fresco lifestyle that the two families enjoy when they are on holiday.

Katrine's favourite space is the outdoor dining area. At dusk, the light changes and the atmosphere is magical. Candles and lanterns are lit and, when the weather allows, they sit out on the terrace long into the night. The occupants of her brother's house are within easy earshot, and during summer, social activities are combined. Young cousins dash

OPPOSITE ABOVE AND BELOW: The outdoor area that lies between the two houses has been kept deliberately open and untamed, retaining a sense of the simple, 'back to nature' way of life that the Danes enjoy.

RIGHT AND ABOVE RIGHT: Areas for preparing food, entertaining and relaxing have all been defined in the open spaces that surround each house, shared by both families.

down to the beach for a swim; a recently acquired dog is an excuse for long walks along the beach and meals are prepared and shared together at either house or on the communal deck of the annexe.

While these houses have been configured to enable social interaction and shared holiday experiences, a final touch is the comfortable hammock that's slung between two trees – a perfect spot to enjoy a few precious hours of solitude before the reassuring sound of children returning from the beach signals the start of another family gathering.

OPPOSITE: Jannik's house, the newer of the two, has been sympathetically designed to reflect the style and feel of the original dwelling, which is now occupied by Katrine. The same 1950s chairs were chosen so as to accommodate large family gatherings.

RIGHT AND BELOW: Large double doors open up to the front and rear of the house onto small decks, one with stunning views of the ocean. Having an outdoor area on both sides of the house means that there is access to sunshine right throughout the day.

sources

UK

Baileys Home & Garden
www.baileyshomeandgarden.com
Perfect pieces for a relaxed home: recycled glassware, nautical floats, coir fenders, driftwood, outdoor furniture and lights.

The Cloth Shop
290 Portobello Road
London W10 5TE
www.theclothshop.net
Large range of fabric including Swedish linens, rag rugs, Indian silk shawls, antique Welsh blankets and other interesting bits and pieces.

Crucial Trading
www.crucial-trading.com
Natural floor coverings and rugs in sisal, seagrass and coir.

Farrow & Ball
www.farrow-ball.com
Historic paint colours.

Francesca's Paints
www.francescaspaints.com
Chalky paints and limewashes in a wonderful range of colours, plus bespoke service.

Garden Trading
www.gardentrading.co.uk
Tasteful items for house and garden, including linen cushions, deckchairs and enamelware.

Ian Mankin
www.ianmankin.co.uk
Ticking fabrics in seaside stripes plus cushions and accessories.

Little Greene
www.littlegreene.co.uk
English heritage paints, with complex pigmentation and depth of colour.

Pebble
www.pebblelondon.com
Stunning range of shells and shell jewellery, coral, glass and wood, sourced from China, India, Thailand, Africa and South America.

RE
www.re-foundobjects.com
Rare, recycled, rescued and restored original and creative products.

Southsea Deckchairs
www.deckchairs.co.uk
Wide range of deckchairs, parasols, windbreaks in bright beach stripes.

Toast
www.toast.co.uk
A selection of natural bed linens, throws, cushions, straw baskets, lanterns and other items for the home.

Thomas Bramwell Collection
www.thomasbramwell.com
Sleek, contemporary outdoor furniture.

The White Company
www.thewhitecompany.com
High-quality bed linen and stylish home accessories, predominantly white and neutrals.

The White Lighthouse
www.thewhitelighthousefurniture.com
A large selection of baskets plus driftwood frames and mirrors.

EUROPE

Emery et Cie
www.emeryetcie.com
Stunning tiles and paints, as well as tableware, fabrics, lighting and rugs.

Merci
111 Boulevard Beaumarchais
75003 Paris
France
www.merci-merci.com
The perfect one-stop shop for eclectic homewares, haberdashery and antiques.

USA

Barn Light Electric
www.barnlightelectric.com
Traditional-style interior and exterior lighting and ceiling fans.

Benjamin Moore paints
www.benjaminmoore.com
Huge selection of colours, many of which fit a coastal palette.

Coastal
7 South Beach Street
Nantucket MA 02554
www.coastalnantucket.com
Vintage home and garden furniture and accessories with a seaside flavour.

John Derian
www.johnderian.com
Wonderful selection of shells, mother of pearl spoons, lanterns, Moroccan ottomans, furniture, textiles and rugs, amongst the well known decoupage collection.

The New General Store
www.thenewgeneralstore.com
A beautifully curated collection of homewares celebrating Long Island style and perfect for simple summer interiors.

Ochre
www.ochrestore.com
Elegant, understated furniture, lighting and homewares, plus art and craft pieces.

Paula Rubenstein
21 Bond Street
New York, NY 10012
www.paularubenstein.com
Antiques and vintage, including ticking fabrics, vintage quilts, natural-dyed linen, ship chains, maritime paintings and photographs.

Restoration Hardware
www.restorationhardware.com
Reclaimed wood coffee tables, natural-fibre rugs, rope-covered chandeliers and much more.

Urban Remains
www.urbanremainschicago.com
A treasure trove of vintage American artefacts and antiques.

business credits

Alex Bates
Founder/Creative Director
Flint & Kent, New York
E: alex@flintandkent.com
www.flintandkent.com
*pages 7 ar, 16 a, 31 bl, 34, 39 br, 47 br,
118–125.*

Hanne Dalsgaard & Henrik Jeppesen
Henrik Jeppesen
Attention Design
www.attdesign.dk
and
Hanne Dalsgaard
Halskov & Dalsgaard Design
www.halskovdalsgaard.dk
*pages 7 br, 10, 19 bl, 33 ar, 33 br, 44 br, 45 br,
47 ar, 60–67.*

Janet Kielley
Interior Design: Janet Kielley Interiors
E: janet@janetkielleyinteriors.com
T: +1 508 332 9261
Architect: Luke & Carrie Thornewill
Thornewill Design
48 Dukes Road
Nantucket Island
MA 02554
T: +1 508 228 9161
E: thornewilldesign@comcast.net
Decorative painting: Christina Wiggins
T: +1 508 221 1159
pages 20 al, 31 br, 35 c, 108–117.

Tine Kjeldesen
www.tinekhome.com
pages 23 l, 35 r, 45 bl, 136–141.

Rick Livingston
Rick Livingston
Period
186 5th Avenue, 2nd floor
New York, NY 10010
T: +1 917 842 7471
www.period-nyc.com
E: rlivingston@period-nyc.com

Location agent for this house:
www.onthemarklocations.com
*pages 7 al, 17, 31 ac, 32, 33 al, 36 al, 39 bl,
44 bl, 84–93.*

Isabel López-Quesada
www.isabellopezquesada.com
Landscape design: Fernando Caruncho
www.fernandocaruncho.com
*8–9, 13 a, 14c, 14 r, 16 bl, 16 br, 19 al, 19 br,
20 ar, 21, 22 al, 23 r, 24 c, 24 r, 25, 26 al, 28 c,
29, 35 l, 37, 39 a, 40 l, 42 l, 42 r, 43 a, 43 bl,
47 al, 47 br, 94–107, 126–135.*

**Jannik Martensen-Larsen and
Helene Blanche**
Jannik Martensen-Larsen:
www.tapet-café.com
*Jannik takes on interior projects for hotels,
restaurants and private houses.*
Helene Blanche:
www.tapet-café.com
*Helene designs Tapet Café's own wallpaper
and fabric collection, represented in the UK
by Tissus d'Helene*
T: +44 (0)20 7352 9977
www.tissusdhelene.co.uk
The collection is also stocked by Liberty
in London: www.liberty.co.uk
pages 19 ar, 150 ar, 152 b, 153–155.

Katrine Martensen-Larsen
www.kmldesign.dk
*pages 11, 36 br, 40 c, 148–150 al, 150 b,
151, 152 a.*

Steve Schappacher and Rhea White
SchappacherWhite LTD
Shelter Island, NY
T: +1 631 749 2675
New York, NY
T: +1 212 279 1675
Enquiries: info@schappacherwhite.com
www.schappacherwhite.com
pages 14 l, 24 l, 26 b, 27 r, 43 br, 142–147.

Cary Tamarkin
Architect
Tamarkin Co.,
www.tamarkinco.com
and
Associate Architect:
Techler Design Group
www.techlerdesign.com
Interior Design:
Suzanne Shaker interiors
www.suzanneshaker.com
*pages 2–3, 13 b, 15, 18, 22 bl, 27 l, 28 l, 28 r,
30, 36 bl, 41, 48–59.*

Robert Young Architects
Robert Young Architecture & Interiors
526 West 26th Street, Suite 616
New York, NY 10001
T: 212-687-6940
E: contact@ryarch.com
www.ryarch.com
Landscape Architecture and Garden
Design: Brady Anderson of
Brady Mitchell Anderson, Ltd.
PO Box 656
57 Church Lane
Bridgehampton, NY 11932
USA
T: +1 631 745 0045
E: office@bmalandscape.com
www.bmalandscape.com
pages 12, 20 b, 22 ar, 22 br, 26 ar, 38, 74–83.

Crena Watson
Crena Watson Photography
T: +44(0)770 343 8888
E: crena@crenawatson.com
www.crenawatson.com
pages 1, 36 ar, 40 r, 68–73.

index

Figures in italics indicate captions.

picture credits

Key: **a** = above, **b** = below, **r** = right, **l** = left, **c** = centre

1 Crena Watson Photographer www.crenawatson.com; **2–3** The home of Cary Tamarkin and Mindy Goldberg on Shelter Island; **7 al** The home of Rick Livingston and Jim Brawders at Quogue, New York on Long Island; **7 ar** Andrew Hoffman & Alex Bates' home on Fire Island; **7 br** The family home of Hanne Dalsgaard & Henrik Jeppesen in Zealand, Denmark; **8–9** The summer home of designer Isabel López-Quesada; **10** The family home of Hanne Dalsgaard & Henrik Jeppesen in Zealand, Denmark; **11** The family home of the stylist and writer Katrine Martensen-Larsen in Zealand, Denmark; **12** Robert Young, Robert Young Architecture & Interiors www.ryarch.com; **13 a** The summer home of designer Isabel López-Quesada; **13 b** The home of Cary Tamarkin and Mindy Goldberg on Shelter Island; **14 l** Designed by Steve Schappacher and Rhea White of SchappacherWhite Ltd; **14 c & r** The summer home of designer Isabel López-Quesada; **15** The home of Cary Tamarkin and Mindy Goldberg on Shelter Island; **16 a** Andrew Hoffman & Alex Bates' home on Fire Island; **16 bl** A guest house in Biarritz designed by Isabel López–Quesada; **16 br** The summer home of designer Isabel López-Quesada; **17** The home of Rick Livingston and Jim Brawders at Quogue, New York on Long Island; **18** The home of Cary Tamarkin and Mindy Goldberg on Shelter Island; **19 al** The summer home of designer Isabel López-Quesada; **19 ar** The summerhouse of Helene Blanche and Jannik Martensen-Larsen, owner of Tapet Café in Copenhagen www.tapet-café.com; **19 bl** The family home of Hanne Dalsgaard & Henrik Jeppesen in Zealand, Denmark; **19 br** The summer home of designer Isabel López-Quesada; **20 al** Interior design: Janet Kielley/Janet Kielley Interiors and Architect: Luke Thornewill/Luke Thornewill Designs; **20 ar** The summer home of designer Isabel López-Quesada; **20 b** Robert Young, Robert Young Architecture & Interiors www.ryarch.com; **21** The summer home of designer Isabel López-Quesada; **22 al** A guest house in Biarritz designed by Isabel López–Quesada; **22 ar** Robert Young, Robert Young Architecture & Interiors www.ryarch.com; **22 bl** The home of Cary Tamarkin and Mindy Goldberg on Shelter Island; **22 br** Robert Young, Robert Young Architecture & Interiors www.ryarch.com; **23 l** The summerhouse of Tine Kjeldesen of www.tinekhome.com in Denmark; **23 r** The summer home of designer Isabel López-Quesada; **24 l** Designed by Steve Schappacher and Rhea White of SchappacherWhite Ltd www.schappacherwhite.com; **24 c & r** The summer home of designer Isabel López-Quesada; **25** The summer home of designer Isabel López-Quesada; **26 al** A guest house in Biarritz designed by Isabel López–Quesada; **26 ar** Robert Young, Robert Young Architecture & Interiors www.ryarch.com; **26 b** Designed by Steve Schappacher and Rhea White of SchappacherWhite Ltd; **27 l** The home of Cary Tamarkin and Mindy Goldberg on Shelter Island; **27 r** Designed by Steve Schappacher and Rhea White of SchappacherWhite Ltd; **28 l & r** The home of Cary Tamarkin and Mindy Goldberg on Shelter Island; **28 c** The summer home of designer Isabel López-Quesada; **29** A guest house in Biarritz designed by Isabel López–Quesada; **30** The home of Cary Tamarkin and Mindy Goldberg on Shelter Island; **31 bl** Andrew Hoffman & Alex Bates' home on Fire Island; **31 ac** The home of Rick Livingston and Jim Brawders at Quogue, New York on Long Island; **31 br** Interior design: Janet Kielley/Janet Kielley Interiors and Architect: Luke Thornewill/Luke Thornewill Designs; **32 & 33 al** The home of Rick Livingston and Jim Brawders at Quogue, New York on Long Island; **33 ar & br** The family home of Hanne Dalsgaard & Henrik

Jeppesen in Zealand, Denmark; **34** Andrew Hoffman & Alex Bates' home on Fire Island; **35 l** The summer home of designer Isabel López-Quesada; **35 c** Interior design: Janet Kielley/Janet Kielley Interiors and Architect: Luke Thornewill/Luke Thornewill Designs; **35 r** The summerhouse of Tine Kjeldesen of www.tinekhome.com in Denmark; **36 al** The home of Rick Livingston and Jim Brawders at Quogue, New York on Long Island; **36 ar** Crena Watson Photographer www.crenawatson.com; **36 bl** The home of Cary Tamarkin and Mindy Goldberg on Shelter Island; **36 br** The family home of the stylist and writer Katrine Martensen-Larsen in Zealand, Denmark; **37** The summer home of designer Isabel López-Quesada; **38** Robert Young, Robert Young Architecture & Interiors www.ryarch.com; **39 a** The summer home of designer Isabel López-Quesada; **39 bl** The home of Rick Livingston and Jim Brawders at Quogue, New York on Long Island; **39 br** Andrew Hoffman & Alex Bates' home on Fire Island; **40 l** The summer home of designer Isabel López-Quesada; **40 c** The family home of the stylist and writer Katrine Martensen-Larsen in Zealand, Denmark; **40 r** Crena Watson Photographer www.crenawatson.com; **41** The home of Cary Tamarkin and Mindy Goldberg on Shelter Island; **42 l** The summer home of designer Isabel López-Quesada; **42 r & 43 a** A guest house in Biarritz designed by Isabel López–Quesada; **43 bl** The summer home of designer Isabel López-Quesada; **43 br** Designed by Steve Schappacher and Rhea White of SchappacherWhite Ltd; **44 bl** The home of Rick Livingston and Jim Brawders at Quogue, New York on Long Island; **44 br** The family home of Hanne Dalsgaard & Henrik Jeppesen in Zealand, Denmark; **45 bl** The summerhouse of Tine Kjeldesen of www.tinekhome.com in Denmark; **45 br** The family home of Hanne Dalsgaard & Henrik Jeppesen in Zealand, Denmark; **46** Andrew Hoffman & Alex Bates' home on Fire Island; **47 al** The summer home of designer Isabel López-Quesada; **47 ar** The family home of Hanne Dalsgaard & Henrik Jeppesen in Zealand, Denmark; **47 bl** Andrew Hoffman & Alex Bates' home on Fire Island; **47 br** The summer home of designer Isabel López-Quesada; **48–59** The home of Cary Tamarkin and Mindy Goldberg on Shelter Island; **60–67** The family home of Hanne Dalsgaard & Henrik Jeppesen in Zealand, Denmark; **68–73** Crena Watson Photographer www.crenawatson.com; **74–83** Robert Young, Robert Young Architecture & Interiors www.ryarch.com; **84–93** The home of Rick Livingston and Jim Brawders at Quogue, New York on Long Island; **94–107** The summer home of designer Isabel López-Quesada; **108–117** Interior design: Janet Kielley/Janet Kielley Interiors and Architect: Luke Thornewill/Luke Thornewill Designs; **118–125** Andrew Hoffman & Alex Bates' home on Fire Island; **126–135** A guest house in Biarritz designed by Isabel López–Quesada; **136–141** The summerhouse of Tine Kjeldesen of www.tinekhome.com in Denmark; **142–147** Designed by Steve Schappacher and Rhea White of SchappacherWhite Ltd; **148–150 al** The family home of the stylist and writer Katrine Martensen-Larsen in Zealand, Denmark; **150 ar** The summerhouse of Helene Blanche and Jannik Martensen-Larsen, owner of Tapet Café in Copenhagen www.tapet-café.com; **150 b–151** The family home of the stylist and writer Katrine Martensen-Larsen in Zealand, Denmark; **152 a** The family home of the stylist and writer Katrine Martensen-Larsen in Zealand, Denmark; **152 b–155** The summerhouse of Helene Blanche and Jannik Martensen-Larsen, owner of Tapet Café in Copenhagen www.tapet-café.com;

acknowledgments

My thanks, first and foremost, go to Earl Carter – not only for taking part in this project, but for capturing all the stunning locations that we were fortunate enough to shoot. I am grateful for his beautiful photography, creative energy, tireless enthusiasm (even on bad weather days) and his willingness to go the extra mile to get the perfect shot. It was, as always, a pleasure to work with him.

Thanks to everyone at Ryland Peters & Small, including Leslie and her design team, Barbara, Jess for securing all our wonderful locations and a special thanks to Annabel for being such a fantastic and patient editor.

Thank you to the wonderful owners, architects and designers who let us shoot their homes and projects, all of whom were extremely hospitable and kind and made such an effort to ensure everything was right for us on the day.

And of course a big thank you to my supportive husband Angus and to Archie, Lily and Harry – for your patience and understanding that this book meant more time away and less time with you, and a busier-than-usual household.